Searching
4 Faith

For Eden,
my delight

Searching
4 Faith

BRIAN DRAPER

A Lion Book
an imprint of
Lion Hudson plc
Mayfield House, 256 Banbury Road,
Oxford OX2 7DH, England
www.lionhudson.com
ISBN 0 7459 5195 3

First edition 2006
10 9 8 7 6 5 4 3 2 1 0

Bible Acknowledgments
pp. 6, 20–21, 22, 26, 29, 36, 44, 49, 50, 51–52, 54,
58, 60, 61, 62, 67, 70, 72, 79, 81, 92, 93, 94, 103, 104,
113, 114, 115, 125 Scripture quotations taken from the
Holy Bible, New International Version, copyright ©
1973, 1978, 1984 International Bible Society. Used by
permission of Zondervan and Hodder & Stoughton
Limited. All rights reserved. The 'NIV' and 'New
International Version' trademarks are registered in the
United States Patent and Trademark Office by
International Bible Society. Use of either trademark
requires the permission of International Bible Society.
UK trademark number 1448790.
pp. 25, 92, 111, 117, 120, 121, 122 Scripture
quotations taken from The Message. Copyright ©
1993, 1994, 1995, 1996, 2000, 2001, 2002. Used
by permission of NavPress Publishing Group.

p. 83 'Jesus Was An Only Son' by Bruce Springsteen.
Copyright © 2005 Bruce Springsteen. Reprinted by
permission. International copyright secured. All rights
reserved.

A catalogue record for this book is available
from the British Library

Typeset in 12/13 Lapidary333 BT
Printed and bound in Singapore

Contents

Preface

We've been
drivin' thru
a desert,
looking for
a life to call
our own.

*Beck,
'Earthquake
Weather'*

The way of Christ is a life-affirming, creative quest to become more fully and more radically human. It refuses to toe the line, surrender to banality, fit in or accept the status quo. It loves life and everything God created; and it hates injustice.

It's not about religion. It's about following Jesus through the streets and alley ways of life in the twenty-first century on a pilgrimage towards the God who is love. This isn't an easy calling, but it is an adventure. It's not a consumerist quick fix, but it yields everlasting results.

This book explores what it means to follow Christ within today's culture. It asks how and why we should, and – at a time when many more of us are searching for spiritual guidance – it offers suggestions for travelling with grace along this path.

Jesus said, 'I am the way and the truth and the life.' It's one of the most startling claims that anyone has made. As we begin to ask what it means to be or to become a follower of Christ, this statement of Jesus (recorded in the Gospel of John 14:6) – incorporating three simple yet profound ideas – will provide us with a road map for the rest of this book's journey. Put simply, if we follow the *way* of Christ, we will discover *truth* that will lead us into *life* itself.

After a brief examination of some old questions that we will ask as we begin our search, we'll think about the first of these ideas, the way, in chapters 1 and 2, and consider what it means to see life and faith as a continuous journey to be travelled. In chapters 3 to 5, we'll look at the search after truth, and how Jesus presented the truth of himself to the world in different ways. Finally, in chapters 6 to 9, we'll consider what it means to find the life that Jesus promises through following him. This will involve honesty and vulnerability as we look at the hard times as well as the good; but along the way of Christ, an exciting and purposeful journey unfolds before us.

I'm not trying to give you an all-encompassing package, or to get you to sign on any dotted line. Instead, this is a reflective journey through those words of Jesus that we can explore together, stopping at points to consider some of the most engaging issues facing us today, such as identity, belonging and purpose.

Jesus didn't command us all to become religious; instead, he said, 'Follow me.' I hope, through this book, that you'll walk with me a short distance along that way. Beyond that, of course, it's up to you…

Go well.

Brian Draper

Introduction

How can we become more… human? How can we live well in a world of flux? How can we live more deeply when we spend so much time in the shallows? Where do we look for guidance?

Skimming the surface is all well and good – but the big questions still bubble away beneath: who am I? Why am I here? Where am I going? How can I understand myself better in the light of God? In this introduction, we start by asking some crucial questions – within a brand new context.

iPod, therefore I am: looking for identity in a changing world

We live in perplexing times. The world around us looks very different from how it did even a few years ago. Culture has splintered into myriad shards of microculture. Technology has both shrunk and stretched our experience of space and time. And life can end up feeling like one great dilemma – especially if you want to do the right thing, to lead a good life.

We are all caught in the tension of life in the global village. While we enjoy the smooth, designer curves of the iPod world, we are also painfully aware that we are draining the earth of its resources. As we buy into the Western consumerist dream, we watch the gap between rich and poor grow. And as we celebrate disposable living, we yearn for something longer lasting.

Amid the confusion, excitement and insecurity of the world we call home, it's clear that a little guidance would go a long way. God knows, we all need some from time to time. Yet no one knows who to believe – the politicians and religious institutions have let us down. 'Trust no one' is the mantra of our times. (At least you won't get hurt.)

And no one knows *what* to believe. At a time when we've got more questions than answers, that's a tough call. More

and more people have set out on a spiritual search, sensing that they yearn for something deeper.

You might prefer to sit down to an organic, slow-cooked feast with companions, not a microwave TV dinner on your own. And yet, as you search for something bigger in life, you find that even spirituality has been put up for sale in the pick-and-mix marketplace of lifestyle choice. It's about being cool, not being called. It's about buying the bestseller, not counting the true cost.

We need to ask some old questions afresh

There comes a point at which our souls need to search beyond even designer spirituality. What are we to do? And where are we to turn? How are we to act? And who are we to follow? Frightening, isn't it – to have all the questions and none of the answers? But it's an honest and a refreshing place to start.

Even seasoned followers of Christ — who sometimes act as if they have all the 'right' answers neatly sewn up — are beginning to ask these questions again as they journey into a new century. It's hard work, but it's also liberating, so long as the searcher goes purposefully after truth and refuses to settle for the quick fix that can be plucked from the shelf.

We are undergoing a seismic shift — caught between an age that is passing and an age that is to come. But we must never stop searching for truth, even when some philosophers say that truth is a lie, a story told by the powerful to back up their version of events. Certainly, truth is not what it used to be — at least not in terms of how we understand it. But we dismiss it at our peril, for the pursuit of truth is what helps to make us human.

We can no longer rely on the old answers, developed over the last 500 years or so in a very different world from the one we now inhabit. The modern, linear, rational world of scientific fact has yielded much that is good. Thank goodness for central heating, painless dentistry and flushing toilets! But we are moving beyond the prevailing philosophical idea that the universe is uniquely secular, bereft of God. More and more ordinary people now admit that we cannot go it alone. The twentieth century — the bloodiest in history — helped put an end to the idea that we were progressing independently of God towards an earthly utopia.

Today, we have to make sense of who we are, why we're here and where we're going from our unique, twenty-first-century perspective. And that calls for patience, diligence and wisdom. It also calls for an openness to the divine, the mysterious, the transcendent and the spiritual that we haven't had for centuries.

That doesn't mean we reject all the answers that the past has to offer. It doesn't mean we cut ourselves off from the ancient traditions or even from modern ways of thinking. All human experience brings wisdom to bear for the journey ahead. But it does mean that we must start thinking about

Where do we go from here? The words are coming out all weird, Where are you now when I need you?

Radiohead, 'The Bends'

the role of spirituality for ourselves. If we wish to nurture our maturity, if we wish to grow up into true, spiritual beings, then we must take responsibility for seeking relevant answers to the old questions.

Who is Jesus?

Those who follow Christ today believe that his life and teaching offer more than just another useful self-help guide to complement the Mind, Body and Spirit shelves of the local bookshop. And they believe that the path of Christ is more than just another lifestyle choice to discuss over a triple macchiato at the local coffeehouse on a Sunday morning.

The way of Christ is a way of life; a journey along the road less travelled. It is no longer signposted as the official religion of state, the highway along which we motor en masse in our search for spiritual enlightenment. Few of us now grow up learning the ancient stories that precede and foretell the birth of Christ. (Could we even list the ten commandments?) Few of us know the stories that Christ told to help unlock the deeper secrets of our life on earth. Few of us could say quite why he lived the way he lived – and why he died the way he died.

But if we are to explore the path that wends from deep in the past, through the presence of today and into the future of the unknown, then Christians believe that we all have to confront a crucial question: who was Jesus? And who *is* Jesus? If we're serious about scratching below the shiny veneer of our playful, postmodern culture, the question must be asked, and it demands a serious response.

'Who do *you* say I am?' Jesus first asked this question of his disciple Peter – a passionate man who nevertheless denied Jesus three times as he was being arrested. It's a question that ever since has cascaded through history, and resonates today. And it's one that always requires a personal response – especially because as you stop to

> Our view of reality is like a map with which to negotiate the terrain of life… The problem of map-making is not that we have to start from scratch, but that if our maps are to be accurate we have to continually revise them.
>
> *M Scott Peck,*
> The Road Less
> Travelled

We live in an age when some people will believe almost everything with no evidence and others believe almost nothing in the face of overwhelming evidence. Jesus has [of course] received the attention of both...

J John,
Jesus, The Life

think, you start to realize that not everything is as it seems.

You might, for example, take a look at some churches and conclude that Christians follow an older man, someone who is cast in the sometimes staid image of its leaders in their lofty pulpits. Yet Jesus was thirty when he began teaching in public and only thirty-three when he died. Christians, in fact, follow a younger man.

I'm no idiot. And I like history. Yet it was only recently that I properly discovered who Che Guevara was. I had known of Guevara as the rebel, the cool guy, the silhouette on the T-shirt. (Today, T-shirts of Guevara are more popular than ever, especially after the film *The Motorcycle Diaries*.) But if you had asked me *why* he was revolting, and where, and how, I'd have struggled. Call me ignorant if you will, but I'm probably not alone in our dumbed-down, consumer society.

How many people have a grasp of who Jesus really was and is? How many people know what he did, and where, and how?

Through which lens do we view Jesus today? As consumers? (Do we buy what he had to say?) As capitalists? (What can you get from following Christ?) As members of a civilised modern society? (Jesus embodies all that is decent about our shared values…)

With stars in our eyes, is it possible for us to look at Jesus without seeing him in terms of fame, in terms of personality and stardom, or as an image or an icon? (And thus, perhaps, as a fading star?)

Is it possible to separate him from the pantheon of the

great and the good – from the company of Ghandi, Martin Luther King and Nelson Mandela, raised to sit at the right hand of Mother Teresa and the left of Princess Diana?

Or perhaps even worse, do we see him as a figurehead for Western politics, pitched against Mohammad for a West versus East showdown?

What *does* Jesus mean to our world? If he is to be anything other than, at best, just another face on just another T-shirt, and, at worst, a symbol of corrupt and divisive religiosity, then we must take his claims, his teachings and his life seriously enough to ask if they have anything to say to us today.

How do we see Jesus? Here's an idea to start with. In Jesus, the Bible suggests, we not only see the human face of the awesome, divine, transcendent God, but we also see the divine face of the model human being. The Bible refers to him as Immanuel, which means 'God with us'. One of us. He not only shared stories. He shared our story.

> Either this man was, and is, the Son of God: or else a madman or something worse... You can shut him up for a fool, you can spit at him and kill him as a demon; or you can fall at his feet and call him Lord and God. But let us not come up with any patronizing nonsense about his being a great human teacher. He has not left that option open to us. He did not intend to.
>
> *C.S. Lewis,*
> The Case for Christianity

What is the church?

As we begin to investigate Christ, we can't help noticing that church seems to be part of the package. It's part of the landscape – a place where fellow travellers stop to rest, encourage each other regularly and worship Christ.

The trouble is, the church, which in fact has a timely message, sometimes finds itself vulnerable to accusations of hypocrisy and outmodedness: 'Christians don't practise what they preach. Christians are out of touch…' It's not *all* true, of course, and there are many different types of churches – some lively, some dull; some inspiring, some less so.

But the church is, after all, filled with ordinary, fallible human beings, trying to make a difference. While they may fall short of the mark, the ideal to which they aspire is high. In fact, the theologian Stanley Hauerwas says that the task of the church is to be 'the kind of community that tells and tells rightly the story of Jesus'. Followers of Christ believe that they are custodians of the greatest story ever told.

It's now the job of churches to rediscover their creative edge, to begin again to capture the imagination of the serious spiritual searcher, and to tell the 2,000-year-old story in a way that makes sense to the twenty-first century.

Nevertheless, that beguiling story has endured for this long, and just as the church must take responsibility for becoming truly artistic, truly creative, truly poetic and truly reflective through its culture and its community, then the spiritual searcher must also play their part in searching out and listening to the story of Christ.

We all sense that following Christ is not about sitting in neat rows and facing the front, especially at a time in which most of us, Christian or not, are frightened of institutions and authority structures. Following Christ does not mean that we must dress in a certain way and conform to a set of cultural standards before we can belong. It does not mean that we must be nice and middleclass in order to be holy.

Following Christ does not mean, either, that we have to deny the music we love to listen to or the books we read – when music and literature can be so powerful, so

15

inspirational. And prayer does not always have to be a spoken or an imagined set of words, at a time when we like to think visually and sensually about life, the universe and everything in it. Our response to and engagement with the creator God can and should be creative.

Following Christ is not exclusively about going to church. Instead, following Christ is about being part of an *inclusive* community, not an exclusive club. It's about being truly counter-cultural, not only subcultural; about making a radical choice, not just another lifestyle choice among many; about understanding that we are walking together on a journey, with humility. We are still travelling – we haven't, as yet, arrived.

Who am I?

As a part of that journey, following Christ is also about asking one of the oldest questions: who am I? Or what does it mean to be human? This is a question that's older than Sartre, Descartes, Aristotle and Plato. It's a question that has occupied our theology and philosophy for millennia. And it's a question you'd have thought we might have answered by now. In fact, we *have* answered it, but in other ages, at other times, in other ways.

We are now asking what it means to be human within a new context: one in which we can play with our identities; in which humans and machines are becoming entangled and entwined; in which we can display multiple personalities with ease, and dispense with the notion of 'integrity'; in which we face the spectre of genetic engineering; in which our identity is wrapped up in our DNA; in which the brand defines the person; in which we can reinvent ourselves whenever we get bored with who we are.

As potential followers of Christ, we can ask the parallel question, what does it mean to be Christian? For to be Christian is about becoming more like Jesus – and thus, more fully human. The person of Jesus takes on a much more dynamic and cutting role in our lives as we explore what it means again to be alive.

'Who am I?' is the question par excellence that makes us human and shows personhood to be an exclusive quality of the human being in the animal world.

John D. Ziziuolas, Being in Communion

In an age when 'image is everything', we can ask: what does it mean to be made in the image of God? The Bible talks about this idea in its opening chapters. Each of us is part of a wider community – we are 'relational' – but we all have unique identities. We are individual and collective beings – and we are not to be judged upon what we look like but on who we are as people. In fact, we all bear the imprint of the God who made us – we all reflect something of his amazing, diverse character – and this bestows upon us a nobility and an honour which we should respect in each other.

At a time when some philosophers say that we're the sum total of our relationships, how do we affirm that we are relational beings while establishing that we are also individuals? What *is* the me of me, the you of you? Where do we begin and end? Will I like the old man that I am set to become? And will I recognize anything of me in his smile, in his walk, in what he's wearing?... In what he believes?

At a time when some say that 'being is becoming', what does it mean to become more like Jesus? What do we have to change about ourselves to do that? And if we do become more like him, what do we lose? Will I still be me?

In an age of constant reinvention, what does it mean to be 'born again'? Is that a fresh start? A mutation? A denial of all that we have been before? An arrival? A departure? How do we hold the tension between shedding our old selves and realizing the life – and life to the full – that Jesus said he had come to offer?

How might we understand ourselves as characters playing their parts in the greatest story ever told?

In the following chapters, we shall examine some of these possibilities. Anyone who is interested in finding out about Christ sets out on a journey. Jesus says, 'Follow me.' We won't reach an immediate arrival, an instant fix. Instead, we start with a departure. A radical departure, some would say, from the oldest of our ways.

> Who am I? This or the other? Am I one person today, and tomorrow another? Am I both at once? Who am I? They mock me, these lonely questions of mine. Whoever I am, Thou knowest, O God, I am thine.
>
> *Dietrich Bonhoeffer*

PART ONE

The Way

Following Christ is not simply an exercise in self-fulfilment. Ultimately, it connects us to something, or Someone, higher — to Someone beyond ourselves, who can bring meaning to an often apparently meaningless existence, and who can bring healing to our brokenness. In these first chapters, we will look at what it means to walk in the way of Christ, on a journey towards a more meaningful life.

CHAPTER 1

'I am the way':
setting out on the path
to God

'Find yourself!' That's the memorable strapline used by the sportswear giant Nike for one of its recent advertising campaigns; and it is, indeed, a motto for today's society. The words tap into our desire to realize our potential, to reach our goals and to become spiritually more in tune with ourselves.

It's a perfectly valid imperative. Some people leave the comfort of their homes to try to find themselves – travelling to deserted places, faraway lands or different cultures. Some try to meditate, or even to detox, as a way of becoming more connected with their inner selves. It's an important exercise, even if we don't always like what we find when we finally get there.

As we go in search of life, however, and try to get deeper, beyond a shallow, popular worldview, the Bible sounds a valuable word of warning. 'Find yourself!' is not necessarily the be-all and end-all of spiritual fulfilment.

There is always a tension between seeking and finding. Jesus commands and promises his followers to 'seek, and you shall find'. But it's not ourselves that we should first set out to discover: it's God.

We must let go

In setting out to find God, we have to leave some things behind. 'Whoever wants to save his life,' Jesus said, 'will lose

Why always this endless quest for God in the silence of our own minds? Instead of seeking God inside our own heads, couldn't we look for him in something as simple as a chance meeting, a bird flying overhead, or the way the wind sings in the autumn leaves? The trick is in being open to see it.

Bill Carter,
Fools Rush In

it, but whoever loses his life for me will find it.' Many Christians find this message tough and even perplexing. Yet Jesus' words – especially within a consumerist, materialistic culture – have a curious, compelling resonance today.

He didn't mean that we literally have to die to gain life – although many Christians are prepared to die in the face of persecution. Instead, he was talking about an attitude of the heart and mind and spirit, one that opposes selfish greed and gain and looks outwards instead, through Christ, to God and to those around us.

These words and others from the life and teaching of Jesus are recorded in the Gospels of Matthew, Mark, Luke and John, and are reflected upon in the New Testament's letters – written by apostles such as Paul – to the early churches that sprung up after Jesus' death. Although Jesus spoke in many straightforward, hard-hitting ways about himself, he also taught in stories, in pictures, through questions and in metaphors. And these methods give us the space to explore his wisdom and calling without necessarily always having to worry about coming up with 'correct' answers.

For Jesus was less interested in debating with and convincing people than in provoking a personal response in them. If we are serious about going deeper in our understanding of him, we need to make space for that question he asked of Peter: 'Who do you say that I am?'

Thankfully, he hasn't left us in the dark, bereft of direction. He said, 'I am the way and the truth and the life.' And this statement contains great wisdom, as we seek to find true life beyond ourselves and true fulfilment within ourselves.

He wanted justice now. He wanted truth now. He wanted world balance now. He raised the storms of demands in his dreams. He raised impenetrable questions. He kept asking: WHY? After eons he asked: WHAT MUST WE DO? And then he asked: HOW DO WE BRING IT ABOUT? Pressing on, he wanted to know: WHEN? Relentlessly, twisting and turning, he demanded: WHAT IS THE BEST WAY? And with a bit more serenity, not drawing back from the inevitable self-confrontation, he asked: WHAT IS THE FIRST STEP?

Ben Okri, The Famished Road

Which path should I choose?

If Jesus is the way, and the spiritual path is not exclusively about finding yourself but about finding God, and if it is not about saving your life but somehow losing it, then we need to step outside of our automatic, consumerist way of thinking while we consider an alternative way of 'being'. We must beware of applying a materialistic mentality to the quest for spiritual help.

Certainly, despite the way 'spirituality' has

been turned into a trendy consumer lifestyle accessory, there *is* an undercurrent which suggests that many people struggle with the weight of choice today in every sphere of life, and crave help and guidance. You only need to look at the groaning shelves of the Mind, Body and Spirit section of any bookshop for evidence. It's hard enough to know which coffee to choose from your local coffeehouse; how much harder, then, to make a choice when it comes to matters of eternal consequence.

Two Australians, Ross Clifford and Philip Johnson, recently wrote a book called *Jesus and the Gods of the New Age*. As Christians, they spent a long time visiting Mind, Body and Spirit fairs – not to try to convert people to the Christian faith but to listen inquisitively to the questions that were on the lips of spiritual searchers. One of the recurring things they heard was this: 'Which path should I choose?'

As travelling companions on the journey of life, Christians have something very special to offer a spiritual

> **This is my truth; tell me yours.**
>
> *Manic Street Preachers*

searcher seeking a path to travel – good news.

However, Jesus did say he was *the way*, and you may have heard Christians interpreting that to mean, rather baldly, that there is *no other way*. There is certainly an element of decisive choice here – after claiming that he is the way, the truth and the life, Jesus also said, 'and no one comes to the Father except through me'. We'll explore that a little further when we come to the matter of 'truth'. But for now, we need to hold the tension between those two words. Jesus is *the* way. But he is also the *way*.

And this last emphasis brings a greater sense of inclusiveness to the table. Now, when people are more open to the spiritual than they have been in centuries, yet more suspicious than ever before of institutions such as the church, there is something important for us all to meditate on.

If we see the Christian faith less as a single package to buy and more as a path to begin wandering, then we can travel together along that road without fear of rejection or intimidation. We can take our time to explore the countryside, the views and the people without feeling like we must believe at once or be damned.

As we look to Jesus, he says, 'Follow me.' We don't simply make a decision. He calls us. And we set out, taking our first steps along the way.

> **Stop and think: first steps**
>
> Think for a moment about how one particular stage of the path can help us to understand more about God, and ourselves: setting out.
>
> Stop, for a few minutes, to imagine the fear and excitement that come with setting out on a big journey. You might have gone on holiday to a place you've never been to before, or set off to attend an interview for a job.

Getting to know the narrow path

Walking a path involves making a conscious choice to enter it, heading purposefully in a certain direction, making progress, making wise choices, watching out for your own safety and that of others, not getting lost, travelling alongside others and arriving at our destination. Christians believe that the path of faith is no senseless journey. Instead, following the way of Christ provides a sense of direction, purpose and even adventure.

And now consider something very different: how defenceless, tiny and fragile a newborn baby is.

The Message, a contemporary version of the Bible, tells us that 'God became flesh and blood, and moved into the neighbourhood' (John 1:14). Christians believe that God became human. And he didn't just parachute in for the mature, teaching stages of his 'ministry'. A woman gave birth to him, and he depended on her for protection, sustenance, nurturing...

God became a child.

So what must it have been like for God to set out on the journey to which he now calls us — to put himself in our hands? It's a simple thing to say, but a deeply profound thing to try to comprehend: God set out on the journey of life.

So consider this image: A God learning to walk. A God

Following the way of Christ provides a sense of direction, purpose and even adventure.

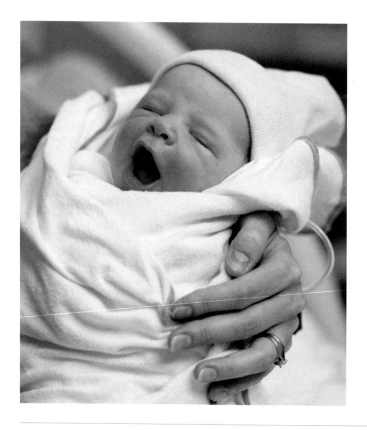

who showed all of us the way, by taking the first steps himself. Literally.

Though this path isn't easy or wide — Jesus himself called it 'narrow' — we *can* walk together along it, whatever label we might put on ourselves and however much 'faith' we think we have, to see where it may lead.

The Bible often contrasts this narrow path with another. The blithe answer 'all roads lead to God' doesn't ever appear. Instead, in the book of Jeremiah (21:8), God says, 'See, I am setting before you the way of life and the way of death.' It is important to seek the road of life as we search, and to acknowledge that other paths, if we are not careful, may not lead us to the best places.

The metaphor of 'the way' or walking on a path is one of the most frequently recurring images in the Bible. In fact, there are over 800 references either to a physical track or to the act of walking in the Bible. This metaphor wends its way through the Bible to the culmination of God's involvement in history. Aside from the literal journeys of so many colourful characters involved in that story (one of the most famous being Moses, who led the Jews out of Egypt in what is known as 'the exodus'), we see the path coming into sharp relief when Isaiah, one of the later Old Testament prophets, called the Israelites to 'prepare the way for the Lord; make straight in the wilderness a highway for our God' (Isaiah 40:3).

That was several hundred years before Jesus was born, but most theologians acknowledge that Isaiah was foretelling the birth of Jesus and the 'ministry' of John the Baptist, who lived at the same time as Jesus and warned people to expect the Messiah. Each of the Gospel writers — Matthew, Mark, Luke and John — cites Isaiah's passage when writing about John the Baptist, who called people out into the desert just before Jesus began his public 'ministry' and baptized them. John was preparing the way of the Lord in the wilderness.

Once Jesus' work got underway, he called a small group of disciples to follow him closely. The *Dictionary of Biblical Imagery* suggests that 'the life of the disciples can aptly be

The life of the disciples can aptly be summed up under the metaphor 'on the road with Jesus'.

Dictionary of Biblical Imagery

Stop and think: reflecting on your own journey

I have to travel to London on the underground twice a week. It's a journey that I don't always relish. But as I head up the escalators, sometimes I try to link my upward and outward journey with the journey that I hope to be making towards God. I try to look at those around me who are sharing my journey, albeit for a few fleeting moments, and I'm reminded of my travelling companions in life. I see adverts flashing past me, a myriad of images all calling for my attention, and try to ask myself how to become more human, not more dehumanized by consumer culture, as I go. I think of the purpose for my journey. I think of those I've left behind, and those whom I'm going to meet. I think of the busyness, and the need to create space within it... I think of the people who are depending on me arriving. And I am able to glimpse that this one journey forms part of a greater whole. There is no such thing as a senseless journey.

Think of a journey you have made, or that you make regularly. What do you enjoy about it? What do you find hard? How might this journey in some way reflect your 'walk of faith' – both metaphorically and literally?

summed up under the metaphor 'on the road with Jesus'. It's little wonder, perhaps, that the earliest followers of Jesus weren't known as Christians at all, but became collectively known as those who belonged to 'the Way'. They had embarked on a literal and metaphorical journey with Jesus.

The good news is that in the story of salvation, God, in Jesus, walked the path himself.

Jesus is recorded walking more than anyone else in the Bible. He showed us the way not so much through a clearly argued set of facts but through a life bravely lived. The way to the Father travels through the Son. It's the way of life itself. And though he's our final destination, he's also our guide and our travelling companion.

Stop and think: life as a ladder?

How do you picture your life? In what way do you see it as a journey? A cultural vignette may help.

When Tony Blair was fifty, his birthday spawned some interesting reflections not just on the implications for the man himself on reaching such a milestone, but on fifty as a milestone that we all hope to reach some day, or may have already reached.

In an article in The Independent, John Walsh (who at the time was 'forty-nine and counting') wrote:

The questions come crowding in on the almost-fifty. How likely am I to die in the next twenty years? How much have I achieved? How healthy am I? Am I attractive to anyone? And lastly, why do I feel a strange mood swing between elation at having survived life, fate and the job market for so long, and a terrible disgruntlement at having stuck at it for all this time?

Walsh went on to talk about the fact that people who are 'fifty-something' now face a greater risk of redundancy, as our culture values the young so much more than the middle-aged and elderly. And he quoted one man in particular, who suffered the experience of being made redundant:

'It's a curious feeling,' reflected Paul the finance director, 'that you've spent so many years climbing the ladder, and all the time it was leaning against the wrong wall.'

Talk about demoralizing! The ladder, surely, is a dominant metaphor of our time. Do we see life as a ladder to be climbed? Is it a helpful image within a culture that places so much emphasis on 'success'? Is there another way of looking at life for this generation?

The Bible offers an alternative metaphor for the sense of upward mobility that most of us crave. The book of Proverbs says that for the wise, 'the path of life leads upward' (15:24). It's an alternative kind of upward – where success isn't measured in terms of career progress or the size of your house. It has more to do with the quality of your relationships – with God, each other, yourself and the planet. And it has an upside-down quality, in which, as Jesus said, 'the first shall be last, and the last shall be first'.

The path of faith in everyday life

In our society, religion and spirituality has been reduced to a private matter. It's something between you and your family, perhaps. It's OK to do it at church on a Sunday, but keep it to yourself for the rest of the week.

This was never meant to be the case, however. Some people – especially sceptics – see religion and spirituality as little more than a curious hobby for the naive, something to do instead of bowls or fishing. Yet followers of Christ believe that their faith is so much more than that. It isn't only for Sunday mornings. It is a calling throughout life, which is just as relevant on Monday morning at work as in church. In a splintering culture, we cannot afford to compartmentalize our lives much further. Following Christ is, instead, about walking with *integrity* – that is, integrating every part of your life in a meaningful, connected way – giving it a narrative, or story, which brings meaning.

If we picture ourselves as following the way of Christ, this will help us to see that every single step we make is significant. Our lives matter to God as a whole, rather than on the whole. The metaphor breaks down the divide, and turns our faith and our life into one continuous path. As Jack Kerouac once wrote in *On the Road*, 'Life is holy, and every moment precious.'

Faith and life can't be separated; life itself is a sacred act – a 'living sacrifice', as the apostle Paul says – and begins to make greater sense as we travel together along the way.

Exchanging the rat race for something better

Life can be hard, and we frequently blame getting caught in the rat race for the fact that we don't have much of a life. In the Bible, Paul talks of life as a different kind of race. 'Run in such a way as to get the prize,' he says. 'I do not run like a man running aimlessly; I do not fight like a man beating the air' (1 Corinthians 9:24–26).

In his letter to the Philippians, he fleshes this idea out: 'Not that I have already obtained all this, or have already been made perfect, but I press on to take hold of that for which Christ Jesus took hold of me… I press on towards the goal to win the prize for which God has called me heavenwards in Christ Jesus.' He presses on, not for personal glory, but for the same reason that, he believes, Christ 'took hold of' him (Philippians 3:12, 14).

Of course, in either race – the rat race or the race run on the path to God – we have in mind a prize. We need to think what it is that we hope to gain from entering either race. What, exactly, is it that we are searching for?

CHAPTER 2

Living in the moment: finding purpose along 'the way'

We're not only bombarded by choice within our consumer culture – which can be bewildering and paralysing enough – but our present age also brings other, peculiar pressures to bear on the simple art of being and becoming human.

In particular, we have lost a sense of the storyline that runs throughout our individual lives, and through the lives of our communities. We are less certain about where we have come from and where we are going – and this, in turn, can have a profoundly negative effect on the way we understand who we are, in the here and now. Some might say that we have, in a sense, lost the plot.

Looking back

Many people in the West feel a lingering and understandable sense of shame about our collective past – we are guilty, by association, of the excesses of imperialism and the degradation of foreign cultures. To make matters worse, these transgressions were often carried out in the name – if not the spirit – of our official religion, Christianity. Many of us feel that a not-so-glorious past has left the West rich and the Rest poor, and we want to distance ourselves from that heritage.

On top of that, the last two centuries failed to deliver the earthly utopia that previous generations believed would

follow naturally from the scientific, philosophical and technological advancements of the modern age. Back in 1851, Prince Albert proudly declared at the opening of London's Great Exhibition that 'nobody who has paid any attention to the peculiar forces of our present era will doubt for a moment that we are living at a period of most wonderful transition, which tends rapidly to accomplish that great end to which indeed all history points – the realization of the unity of mankind'.

Well, that time of transition did not deliver the 'unity of mankind'; instead it yielded the bloodiest period of history known to the human race, culminating in two world wars and at least one holocaust in the twentieth century.

Understandably, rather than sensing an ongoing connection with previous generations, many of us today have grown up unsure of our relationship to the past, believing that those preceding us have handed us a poisoned chalice instead of the key to the future.

As one character in Douglas Coupland's best-selling cult classic *Generation X* puts it, 'I want to throttle them for blithely handing over the world to us like so much skid-marked underwear.'

Over the last few years, some people have begun to declare themselves 'post' modern – rejecting what has gone before in terms of the scientific, rational ideologies that developed through the last two or three hundred years, and in particular, the misguided idea of progress.

What do we have to look forward to?

With the past consigned to history, many people have also grown up with little faith in the future – at times, they have not even been sure whether or not they would have one. Television programmes in the seventies and eighties informed the viewing public what to do in the event of a nuclear war – how to build a bomb-proof shelter behind your settee, for example, and other useful, terrifying pieces of not-so-trivia. As schoolchildren, we would discuss what we would do – and who we'd do it with – if and when we heard the four-minute warning sound...

Today, plenty of other things contribute to the growing sense that we may not have much of a future to look forward to: global warming and the threat of environmental catastrophe; terrorism and the clash of civilizations; even fear of a meteorite smashing into the earth.

Welcome to the twenty-first century. We are all immigrants to a new territory.

Douglas Rushkoff, Children of Chaos

Trapped in the present

And the result? Cut adrift from the past and bereft of a meaningful and optimistic sense of the future, we find ourselves becalmed, like a sailing boat with no wind, in the present. We fear an empty future and swap a sense of hope and purpose for a life of cheaper thrills.

Another metaphor might help us to explore this idea further – the *perpetual adolescent.*

Today, we start adolescence earlier and keep it going for as long as possible. We sexualize our children from an early age, with clothes and make-up, boy bands and girl bands and teen

magazines specifically designed for the target market known as 'tweenagers' – and in doing so, we begin to rob our children of the sacredness of childhood along the way.

At the same time, those of us who are older try to stave off responsibility for as long as possible, extending adolescence into our twenties and thirties. Some manage to take it further still. Society has a name for us too: 'kidults'. The idea is to maintain a life of fun and experience, without becoming trapped by a mortgage, career or spouse – in other words, by the things our parents' generation saw as the path to a successful life (until they got divorced and sold the house to split the proceeds…)

Our popular culture celebrates the cult of youth; meanwhile, those who have gained greater life experience and accumulated deeper wisdom get sidelined because they're not cool enough to be on TV. Surely it's not good for us to become a culture of adolescents? If we don't watch

'It's a curious feeling', reflected Paul the finance director, 'that you've spent so many years climbing the ladder, and all the time it was leaning against the wrong wall.'

John Walsh,
The Independent

out, we will never grow up. We will never go deeper. We will never move on into a future we can all help to shape.

Without a story, we lose our direction

Douglas Coupland identified this cultural malaise in *Generation X*. In one scene, his characters are sat around a fire, talking about life — and in particular, their need to get one:

'We really don't have any values, any absolutes. We've always manoeuvred our values to suit our immediate purposes. There's nothing large in our lives... Instead of serving a higher purpose, we've always been more concerned with developing our "personalities" — and with being "free".'

They continue, 'It's not healthy to live as a succession of isolated little cool moments. Either our lives become stories, or there's just no way to get through them.'

Coupland calls this loss of story — the lack of something bigger in our lives — 'denarration'. And denarration, he says, is the technical way of saying, 'not having a life'.

We are all characters in God's story

We'll explore, a little later, what Jesus meant when he said that he had come to bring us life, and 'life to the full'. For now, however, it is important to acknowledge that as travellers along the way, followers of Christ are set to gain a unique perspective by participating in a historic storyline. Christians believe it's not just a great read — they are, in fact, characters within the greatest story ever told, human beings who are called to play their own part in an ongoing plot of cosmic dimensions.

They can see, in their sacred text the Bible, how they connect to the past — all the way back to the first communities who walked the earth. And the Bible, although it contains many genres of writing by many authors, and many different people and settings, has a unifying theme – the story of God's creation and restoration of life on our planet. It comes to a climax in the incarnation – when God 'became flesh and blood and moved into the neighbourhood' as Jesus. Jesus lived among us, and the New Testament records that he was put to death in order, somehow, to save the human race and the rest of God's creation. But the story doesn't finish there.

Followers of Christ believe that Jesus was raised from the dead, three days after his crucifixion. He was seen by many people after his resurrection, and the Gospel of John tells how Jesus even ate with his disciples again one memorable, moving morning when he cooked them a fish breakfast by Lake Galilee. He was not a ghost, but raised in body as well as spirit.

And so, because of Jesus' life, death and resurrection, we are also offered a real stake in a hopeful future. While the human race is not (and never will be) 'improving' or 'progressing' as the scientists and philosophers of modernity once believed, nevertheless the story continues. As well as offering us everlasting life through Jesus, the Bible promises that *all* things will be made new and that in time, there will be a new heaven and a new earth. Although no one is quite certain how this will happen and what form it will take, Christians understand that God's physical creation – the world around us – will also experience a renewing, a 'resurrection', when God will restore 'all things' to how they once were and how they should be. The book of Isaiah looks forward to the day when 'the lion shall lie down with the lamb', which is a poetic way of saying that the violence of nature will go, and all things – animals, plants and people – will find their relationships with each other and God fully restored.

Why am I always on a plane or a fast train?

Oh what a world my parents gave me.

Always travellin' but not in love Still I think I'm doin' fine.

Wouldn't it be a lovely headline:

'Life is Beautiful' on a New York Times.

Rufus Wainwright, 'Oh what a world'

Moving forwards in faith

Augustine once suggested that 'faith is to believe what you do not see; the reward of this faith is to see what you believe'. Several hundred years later, the rock star Bono of U2 put it another way in the song 'Walk On': 'I'm packing a suitcase for a place none of us has been – a place that has to be believed to be seen.'

Faith in the future can help bring meaning, identity and purpose to the present. Not that everything is made crystal clear to any of us; the apostle Paul says that we still only see 'through a glass darkly' – like squinting through fog. Nevertheless, we have a hope: and so, there is no need to remain as a culture of perpetual adolescents, afraid to grow up and take responsibility for life, afraid to grow old and face the long goodbye of death.

It is not a matter of sitting passively, waiting for our world to start or end. Instead, we are called to become co-creators with God of our own stories – actively working and walking with him to help to change our own future and that of others, for good.

> **Faith is being sure of what we hope for and certain of what we do not see.**
>
> *Hebrews 11:1*

Forgiving the past

Yet before we continue walking, we have to deal with our past. We cannot turn our backs on it completely, for it has made us who we are today. Yet we can face up to what's gone before and resolve to create a brighter future. Once again, as we travel along the way and consider our journey of life and faith to be mysteriously and inextricably intertwined, we can look back and see that we have passed certain milestones along our path. Some may have been positive and happy; others, negative and painful. Some we may have travelled past alone; others, we have reached in the company of friends, lovers, teachers, family and work colleagues. Some we may have noticed passing; others may have passed us by...

God is able to forgive any of those things that seem to us to be unforgivable. (We'll look more at the idea of personal transformation – and repentance – in chapter 6.) Christians believe that through Jesus' life and death, something deeply mysterious and profound shattered the structure of the cosmos as we knew it. Evil was vanquished. Death,

It's the end of
the world as we
know it.

REM,
'It's the End of
the World (as We
Know It')

somehow, was conquered. This means that anyone can now experience forgiveness and the restoration of their relationships – with themselves, each other, God and the universe. They can begin to move on.

Learning to live now

When someone becomes a follower of Christ, it's a wonderful 'arrival'. But it's also a departure into a new life. The old ways are gone, but not forgotten. The new life is starting, but not perfected. We are not treading water, waiting for life after death. As one Christian charity says so brilliantly, 'we believe in life before death'; and we are learning what it means to live more fully, right here, right now. This process won't be completed until we are fully reunited with God, on the other side of death, in a physical resurrection – but the journey starts here.

Remember Douglas Coupland's comment in *Generation X*: 'It's not healthy to live as a succession of isolated little cool moments. Either our lives become stories, or there's just no way to get through them.' If we're not careful, without a sense of purpose, of something bigger, we can end up living from moment to moment, *end of story*. We can end up living *for* the moment, rather than perfecting the art of living *in* the moment. For there *is* a difference.

If we live *for* the moment, we constantly strain forwards, looking for the next eventful episode that can help us construct some form of meaningful story for ourselves. And in so doing, we manage to devalue the sacredness of the present.

It's often boredom – in the absence of purpose – that propels us forwards in the pursuit of sensation; and boredom violates the gift of life that we have been given to treasure. Stillness is very different from boredom.

Another thing that stops us living within the moment is our desire to avoid pain. We've become expert at this, and so we're afraid when pain creeps up on us. In particular, our culture has tried to numb the pain that we feel in forgetting who we are and where we are going. We prefer to amuse ourselves to death, or at least to drug ourselves, rather than confront the existential angst of such loss.

But in stopping to embrace the moment, however painful that may sometimes be, we might yet learn to live – within the present. Instead of waiting for reality to kick in through a series of 'cool' events, our humanity expands, broadens and deepens as we try to embrace the reality of the present.

There are ways of training ourselves to do this, and perhaps contemplation or meditation is a way of consciously slowing ourselves down in this fast-forward culture. The Christian mystic Thomas Merton once described contemplation as 'a sudden gift of awareness, an awakening to the Real within all that is real'. He understood it very simply as 'spontaneous awe at the sacredness of life, of being'.

> I'm 35 years old, and I own a tiny failing business, and my friends don't seem to be friends at all but people whose phone numbers I haven't lost. And if I went back to sleep and slept for 40 years and woke up without any teeth to the sound of Melody Radio in an old people's home, I wouldn't worry that much, because the worst of life, i.e. the rest of it, would be over.
>
> *Nick Hornby,*
> High Fidelity

A step in every moment

In *The Sacred Journey*, Mike Riddell introduces a useful metaphor that helps us to think about the constant flow of the present through our lives. He writes about the 'blade of the moment', which cuts the past and the future in two.

> When we learn to become fully present in every instant, we discover that there are opportunities and choices immediately before us which will determine both our past and our future.
>
> Here on the sharp blade of the moment lie opportunities to create and to love. Equally present are the possibilities of abuse and cruelty. In the capsule of experience which is given to us each instant, we determine who we are and what is significant to us. The whole of our lives is presented to us in the moment, and each moment is an intersection with eternity in which we decide our destiny and are offered the grace of becoming. All else is illusion.

This is the language of choice. Yet, in the way of Christ, it is, as always, a different kind of choice from the consumerism that surrounds us. Instead of worrying about which brand to buy, we are faced with choices about life, about goodness, about consequences, every moment of every day, and we are called to make wise, different choices.

One of those choices involves giving and receiving. Jesus said, 'Freely you have received, freely give' (Matthew 10:8). Riddell also talks of the search we make for God's 'self-giving love'. We are all, somehow, searching for the freedom to be loved for who we are, and when we find that self-giving love, we are then released to embark on the journey to become the people God intended us to be. Self-giving love is infectious and spontaneous. As we discover that we are loved unconditionally by God, we should find that self-giving love flows outwards through us towards others. It becomes a source of joy, to begin giving up our own lives for the sake of others. 'And in this simple act,' writes Riddell, 'we discover the meaning of love, in all its joy and pain, and the divine spirit flows through us.'

Stop and think: labyrinth – an exercise in walking with God

I was part of a group experimenting with new forms of Christian worship, and we borrowed an idea from a medieval spiritual exercise called the labyrinth. It's a walking meditation, based on an ancient form of pre-Christian ritual that was later adopted by Christians in their own worship. The earliest remaining example can be seen – and walked – in Chartres Cathedral.

It looks like a maze, but in fact it is a circular path that leads you on an 'inward journey' towards a central space, then out again. You can't go wrong. Labyrinths come in all sorts of shapes and sizes, and their paths may be hewn in stone, marked out by string or carved by a stick in the sand. They are simple, contemplative aids to worship.

The labyrinth symbolizes the walk with God. You walk it slowly and take at least half an hour to complete it. In the version we designed, as you walk you are encouraged at various points to stop and think about a range of things: faith as a journey; your fellow travelling companions; the symbolism of light and dark; your identity as a human being in relation to yourself, others, the creation and God; contemporary culture; the ecological issues facing the planet today; issues of forgiveness and being forgiven...

It is usually set in a darkened room, with ambient music playing and voiceovers and visuals on TV screens and banners. It is primarily a relaxed, spiritual space in which to spend an hour or two sitting, kneeling, lying, praying, thinking and worshipping. Not everyone can go through the labyrinth at once, so we have three 'stations' outside of the path where people can model clay, construct prayer trees, paint, write or plant seeds. These allow people to explore specifically their relationships to others, themselves and the planet.

Within the labyrinth itself, which serves as the 'relating to God' station, we use small candles to help symbolize our own faith and experience of God, as we prepare to come before him (with our candles unlit). God is symbolized as a larger candle in the central space.

Once we have taken the time to pray and think and experience his love, we then light our own candles and take them, symbolically again, on the outward journey into the world – drawing on the prologue from John's Gospel, which says that 'the true light which gives light to every person was coming into the world'. The outward journey in particular emphasizes the theological and practical theme of God becoming human, which is so beautifully rendered in the prologue.

Throughout the labyrinth, the concept of *journey* is uppermost. It underlines the idea that conversion is a process – one that is punctuated by moments of joy and crisis – not a one-off, be-all-and-end-all commitment.

So Christians and those who would not describe themselves as such can walk the labyrinth alongside one another; it is accessible to all who are on a journey.

The labyrinth is a good example (and a physical demonstration) of how you can explore the Christian faith without intimidation or duress. We all need space for safe, inspiring and authentic spiritual exploration. It helps pilgrims to enact their walk with God visually, and physically and spiritually move closer to the divine.

The way of Christ is open

There are many new, diverse ways in which people are exploring and expressing the Christian story today. These ways promote openness, inclusiveness, curiosity, calm, contemplation and creativity. As we begin to walk literally and metaphorically on our journey with God and each other, the words of Mike Riddell might inspire us forwards, out of the boredom and numbness, and help us to move on in the present with excitement. 'The Way of Christ, out of which I live,' he writes, 'is not a closed perspective but an open one. It suggests a continuous surging creative drive at work in the world, which is relentlessly transforming life.'

PART TWO

The Truth

What is truth? And what did Jesus mean by saying that he was 'the truth'? In the next three chapters, we look at how truth has become a dirty word in today's culture, and how Jesus transforms the idea. Embodied in him, truth is no longer a weapon for the powerful, but the way to God for all who search after it.

CHAPTER THREE

'I am the truth': discovering the truth of Jesus in today's world

Pilate [asked], 'It was your people and your chief priests who handed you over to me. What is it you have done?'

Jesus said, 'My kingdom is not of this world. If it were, my servants would fight to prevent my arrest by the Jews. But now my kingdom is from another place.'

'You are a king, then!' said Pilate.

Jesus answered, 'You are right in saying I am a king. In fact, for this reason I was born, and for this I came into the world, to testify to the truth. Everyone on the side of truth listens to me.'

'What is truth?' Pilate asked.

John 18:35–38

We all must ask: what is truth?

Stop and think: what is truth?

Stop for a moment and ask yourself the question, What is truth? If you look up the word 'truth' in a dictionary, does it refer you to anything more than another set of words? How does your idea of truth compare with that of someone you find yourself completely opposed to?

It's hard to side with a man like Pontius Pilate, so famous for 'washing his hands' of Jesus prior to the crucifixion. Yet his final question in the exchange above — 'What is truth?' — is an important one. We've probably all asked it, or thought it, at different stages in our life. We don't know whether Pilate was being cynical, sceptical or genuinely curious, but it makes us think: what was he looking for? And why, if Jesus was who he claimed to be, couldn't Pilate see the truth, even though it was staring him in the face?

Our job is not to second-guess the infamous Roman governor; it is, instead, to take seriously this moment in the life of Christ — one that, in the white-hot tension of a terrifying ordeal, raises the question of truth and recalls the words that Jesus used earlier in his life to describe who he was and why he was here: 'I am the way and the *truth* and the life.'

Real 'truth' stands firm in the face of adversity, and Jesus remained unwavering about who he was, even in the face of death. However, the concept of truth itself has often been a slippery idea for humans to grasp; it was back then and it remains so today.

In fact, in the last two decades or so, many philosophers, writers, artists, protestors, spiritual searchers and plain, ordinary people have again been asking, what is truth? And though this question is as old as Pilate and Jesus, it should be asked again and again if we are serious about searching out the heart of life itself.

Men occasionally stumble over the truth, but most of them pick themselves up and hurry off as if nothing ever happened.

Winston Churchill

We've reached a moment of truth… for truth

We live at a uniquely challenging and pivotal time in history; a time when truth itself is up for grabs as we begin to question the way people have moulded it, melded it and made it up over the last 300 years. Around the time of the Enlightenment, the philosophers, academics and scientists in the West began to see truth as 'absolute' – set in stone. They believed they could take anything in the world, examine it and find out exactly how it worked. Through scientific and philosophical endeavour, anyone could discover truth, write it down in a neutral and objective way and preserve it for all time. No argument.

At the same time, we decided that we no longer needed God to explain all the mysteries of life, because we were solving them on our own. The truth demystified our universe; sadly, it also left it empty of spiritual awe and wonderment.

To an extent, of course, the 'modern' thinkers were right. Scientific discovery did yield certain laws by which the

universe truly seemed to behave. Today, we can build aeroplanes and they will, on the whole, stay up in the air. However, it's one thing to build an aircraft using human knowledge and ability, and quite another to build a philosophy based on the idea that our own knowledge and ability will solve our metaphysical problems, making us masters of our ultimate destiny.

For a start, the idea of scientific *certainty* has always been tenuous, as scientists themselves are forever discovering that their previous theories weren't fully right. For example, when Einstein published his theory of relativity in 1905, he turned the Newtonian world of physics upside down and inside out.

And another problem presented itself when it came to the sanctity of human knowledge: 'truth' was always assigned from the perspective of the powerful and victorious. Those in power wrote history according to their own way of seeing things – with rarely much thought for the other characters involved. The voiceless couldn't tell their own story; the marginalized couldn't report on how they saw the world.

'Truth' was at best one-sided, and at worst, a lie. Society became deeply suspicious of people who preached 'the truth' but didn't live according to it – whether they were politicians or religious leaders.

There are many more wrong answers than right ones, and they are easier to find.

Michael Friedlander

Beginning to understand truth differently

Gradually, we began to wake up and smell the fairly traded coffee. We understood that it was harder to speak of objective truth than we realized, because two different people could observe the same thing, the same incident, the same text, in two different ways. (Try asking opposing soccer fans whether that really *was* a penalty…) Recently, we have come to understand truth as something that is agreed upon by a number of people – arrived at by social consensus; but even then, we have to acknowledge that there might be conflicting ideas about which consensus is right.

Truth is a story we tell each other about the nature of life around us. But to claim we have exclusive, unmediated access to the truth, the whole truth and nothing but the truth is an increasingly difficult thing to do. When George W. Bush announced, just hours before the USA invaded Iraq, that 'this is a moment of truth for the world', the cynic in us replied, 'Truth on whose terms?'

We should thank God for such a challenge to the idea of truth within our culture, even though it has left us all with a very difficult task.

We must never stop searching for the truth

The task is to keep searching for the truth – for not to do so would be to devalue our humanity. We cannot stand back, shrug our shoulders and say, 'It doesn't matter.' Whether it's the truth about who really committed a crime, the truth about how a friend is really feeling, the truth about how many people are really dying from Aids/HIV in the developing world or the truth about how the universe was

really breathed into life, we have to remain curious about the world around us. The truth must come out – and we hope it comes out on the side of the people who need it most: poor people, the oppressed, the marginalized, the hurting, the homeless and the hopeless.

The truth is still out there. But we must handle it in a different way. We must handle it with care, humility and compassion.

Truth is found in relationship with God

Followers of Christ believe that their particular story is 'true', not exclusively for them but for anyone who is willing to listen; for those, as Jesus said, 'who have ears to hear'. But things have changed in the way that they seek to present the Christian story: it's not about wanting to gain power, to pack out the churches, to force everyone to like and listen to them.

Instead, it's about *living* truth – not just talking a good talk about forgiveness, light, love, peace and reconciliation, but walking it too. It's about letting the whispering voices of the oppressed be heard above the booming of the powerful. The gospel of Christ turns truth, as we know it, on its head.

According to Jesus, truth is less about a written set of words and more about a relationship. The Word, as the Bible says, became flesh and blood. Sin, then, is less about breaking the words of the law and more about being outside of a relationship with the person of Christ. And truth is less about believing exactly the same thing as everyone else, and more about being in the right kind of relationship with Jesus, the Word.

Jesus said that he was the way, the truth and the life. He also declared that 'if you hold to [his] teaching, you are really [his] disciples. Then you will know the truth, and the truth will set you free' (John 8:31–32).

And this, surely, is the litmus test. Truth is fleshed out

> Do you believe
> In what you see?
> Everyone's
> saying different
> things to me,
> different things
> to me.
>
> *Zero 7,*
> *'In the Waiting*
> *Line'*

49

Stop and think: loving God, loving others

You might like to sit where you can see other people. Ask yourself, what does it mean to love God, and to love my neighbour as myself? How might I love my neighbour in a way that I, too, would love to be loved? You might like to write down one thing that you think you could do to love your neighbour: encourage a work colleague, surprise someone with a treat, bury an argument or be the first to say sorry.

through a relationship; and if Jesus is right, then the truth *will* liberate us. But it's not a passive acceptance of a free gift or prize. The challenge is to follow Jesus along a narrow path and to hold to his teaching. That's the way we will find the truth in our lives, which is not waiting to be discovered at all, but waiting to be created, through a way of living and loving that sets us free to become the people that God created us to be.

Truth in the teaching of Jesus

So, what is the teaching of Jesus? Although more books have been written about him than any other person in history, his teaching can in fact be summed up very, very simply. You can read the summary in a story in the Bible (Luke 10:25–28), when an expert in the Jewish law came up to Jesus and asked him a timeless question: 'What must I do to inherit eternal life?'

Jesus answered in the way he often did – with another question:

'What is written in the Law?' he replied. 'How do you read it?'

[The man] answered, 'Love the Lord your God with all your heart and with all your soul and with all your strength and with all your mind'; and, 'Love your neighbour as yourself.'

'You have answered correctly,' Jesus replied. 'Do this and you will live.'

That is the essence, if you like, of becoming more fully human, as a follower of Christ. It is the brand. The core ethic. Love God, and your neighbour as yourself. All else is mere detail.

Stories teach about truth

But we must work these details out together, and for ourselves, in humility and encouragement and according to the words and deeds of Jesus. Jesus taught in many different ways, and the exchange we have followed so far between the legal expert and Jesus led on, in fact, to one of the best-known stories in the Bible. Having asked Jesus what he must do to inherit eternal life, the legal expert then asked Jesus another question: 'Who is my neighbour?'

It's a good question. And good questions can help us to edge nearer the truth. We should never be afraid to ask them. In life, we might prefer to have more answers than questions; though in faith, we should feel comfortable holding the questions. Who am I? Where am I going? Questions drive us onwards towards the truth; if we believe we have all the right answers, then we cease to grow. If we think we've arrived, we no longer continue the journey. If we stop asking the questions, we stagnate.

The good news is that Jesus answers us in such a way that we can keep going deeper. He did not respond to the legal expert with a carefully argued treatise on neighbourliness. Instead, he told a story that will have shocked and perhaps offended many who were listening. The story was the parable of the Good Samaritan. Samaritans were enemies of the Jews. The idea of a 'good' Samaritan was foreign in every way. Yet Jesus, a Jew, told this story to his Jewish listeners:

'A man was going down from Jerusalem to Jericho, when he fell into the hands of robbers. They stripped him of his clothes, beat him and went away, leaving him half

> **Stop and think: who's my neighbour?**
>
> In a quiet moment, read the story of the Good Samaritan and, even if you think you know it, try to think about one thing that you haven't noticed before. Perhaps you might like to imagine you are a child, hearing the story for the first time. In order to set it within a contemporary context, you might like to ask the question, 'Who is my neighbour in the global village?' Consider how you may not know the names of the people who live on your street, but you do know of thousands of people who are, for example, dying from starvation in various parts of the world – far away, yet so close.

dead. A priest happened to be going down the same road, and when he saw the man, he passed by on the other side. So too, a Levite, when he came to the place and saw him, passed by on the other side. But a Samaritan, as he travelled, came where the man was; and when he saw him, he took pity on him. He went to him and bandaged his wounds, pouring on oil and wine. Then he put the man on his own donkey, took him to an inn and took care of him. The next day he took out two silver coins and gave them to the innkeeper. 'Look after him,' he said, 'and when I return, I will reimburse you for any extra expense you may have.'

'Which of these three do you think was a neighbour to the man who fell into the hands of robbers?'

Luke 10:30–36

Open to interpretation

Jesus frequently told stories of almost childlike simplicity, and yet these stories ring true to this day. The parable of the Prodigal Son, for example, is one that you can explore time and time again – even if you think you know what it means already. The parable of the Good Samaritan is another famous story that rewards continued reflection. The longer you spend on it, the deeper you can go.

A parable may convey truth to the listener or reader in different ways, and on different levels, according to who is doing the reading and listening. There is not, necessarily, a right or wrong meaning, although it is important for any contemporary reader to respect the genre and the cultural background of the stories, and to pay attention to any scholar who can help set the scene. Careful study always brings its benefits.

Jesus left many of his parables open-ended. Our tendency, perhaps, is to close down stories by trying to explain their meaning (especially to children, who approach them with such wide-eyed wonder) – to nail down the truth, the moral of the tale, and thus to drain the story of its power, its narrative, its tension. But in leaving them – and himself – open to interpretation, Jesus introduced artistry to the task of teaching and living. He invites us to respond to his teaching personally, and his stories ask that we take responsibility for ignoring or exploring the life-changing potential that they carry.

Jesus spoke the truth in other ways

Jesus taught in other ways too: through preaching, through metaphors and through actions.

Some of his most famous words are to be found in what is known as the Sermon on the Mount. In the Gospels, we are told that while he was teaching and preaching around Galilee, he began to attract large crowds. Faced one day with yet another big following, Jesus went up a mountainside and sat down, perhaps to escape the attention. His disciples came to him, and he began teaching them, saying:

> 'Blessed are the poor in spirit, for theirs is the kingdom of heaven. Blessed are those who mourn, for they will be comforted. Blessed are the meek, for they will inherit the earth. Blessed are those who hunger and thirst for righteousness, for they will be filled. Blessed are the merciful, for they will be shown mercy. Blessed are the pure in heart, for they will see God. Blessed are the peacemakers, for they will be called sons of God. Blessed are those who are persecuted because of righteousness, for theirs is the kingdom of heaven.'
> *Matthew 5:3–10*

Is it my imagination or have I finally found something worth looking for?

Oasis, 'Cigarettes and Alcohol'

Many people who wouldn't even describe themselves as 'Christian' have drawn deep inspiration from these words, which conjure a vision of a very different world. It's a world to come, yet a world we are called to help bring into being. It's a world apart from our own, a world of the now-and-the-not-yet. Jesus is redrawing the boundaries, creating an upside-down kingdom in which the losers become the winners and the last, the first.

The Sermon on the Mount is a useful measuring rod by which to see whether a follower of Christ is really who they claim to be. They might speak flighty words, or claim the name of Christ for the actions they perpetrate; but if they're not trying to live according to Jesus' words (however much we all ultimately fail to do so), their faith is not fleshed out in love; their truth does not stand the test.

When you begin to follow Jesus Christ, you start to glimpse that 'truth' is not the conventional wisdom of the world – the me-first, protect-your-assets mentality that springs naturally from the human heart. The truth can be hard to bear, because it demands sacrifice, strength, courage and conviction. But the truth will stand firm, and it will, we are promised, set us free.

CHAPTER 4

The truth became flesh: how Jesus' life speaks to us

How can we talk about God in words alone? How can we speak of the divine creator of a boundless universe, which sparkles with a billion stars, using human language? At best, our words fail to do God justice. At worst, they ensnare God and misrepresent him; they reduce and confine him. In one sense, God is all that the Bible says about him. And yet he is also more. We couldn't take it in, and neither should we want to. But the radical and perverse idea of the gospel – the 'good news' – is that God became flesh and blood, and took on human form, so that we could see and know him, and crucially, so we could *relate* to him – once and forever.

How did Jesus cope with talking about himself to those who began to follow him? How did he teach everyday people, in everyday language, about the very secrets of the universe?

Metaphorical language opens avenues to truth

As we have seen, Jesus spoke in parables and straight-talking sermons. But he also sketched many pictures with words. He knew and appreciated the power of the simplest metaphor – he had to, in fact, because he was frequently making claims about himself that went beyond the bounds of ordinary human thought and language. Jesus couldn't speak scientifically or in straight facts all the time about who he was, where he came from and where he was taking us. It was too big, too revolutionary, too out of this world. So he used images and metaphors to help us understand more about himself, as any good teacher would.

It's a testament to the power of his teaching and to the potency of the images he used that many of us still know about them today and can explore them for ourselves. Just as the people who were following him around had to consider his words and take responsibility for their own responses, so do we, here and now, in the twenty-first century. For Jesus' teaching style not only gives us the tools by which to live better lives; it also demands that we consider who he was and is, and what he means in relation to us today.

Using pictures to describe reality

One of Jesus' most famous series of sayings about himself is recorded in the Gospel of John. He often spoke about himself to his followers by starting with the words, 'I am…'. This was a not-so-subtle way, in the first century AD, of equating himself with the God of the Israelites, who was known to them as *Yahweh*, or 'I am'. It was deliberate on Jesus' part, leaving those who heard him with little option but to accept or reject his divine association with the Almighty. Even though he spoke in pictures and parables, his teaching carried great force and left little room for compromise. Jesus was not suggesting that he was just a good man with some spiritual enlightenment to offer. He wasn't claiming that he was just another prophet, in the line of Israel's other great prophets. His teaching had such a radical edge that it cut through his listeners like a knife – dividing all who heard him speak. After all, he said he was the Son of God.

Jesus completed his 'I am' sayings with different images or metaphors to help those with 'ears to hear' reflect more effectively upon what he was trying to say about himself and about the world that God was going to create through him (he called this God's 'kingdom'). He used images that were especially pertinent to the time. But most have a universal quality that means they remain vital within our own time and space.

Reality leaves a lot to the imagination.

John Lennon

Feeding on the bread of life

Take one of Jesus' most famous sayings. He said, 'I am the bread of life.' The story goes like this: he was followed by a vast crowd. He worked some amazing miracles and they began to think he might be the man to save their people – the Messiah, in other words. Jesus saw the great, hungry crowd and knew he had a chance to feed them in body *and* soul. So, miraculously, he turned a little boy's packed lunch of five loaves and two fishes into a feast that was big enough to feed over 5,000 – with plenty left over.

The next day, the crowd went looking for him again, and he used the incredible episode to teach them (John 6:25–59). He said they came looking for him because the day before they had eaten their fill. He told them not to 'work for food that spoils, but for food that endures to eternal life… The bread of God is he who comes down from heaven and gives life to the world... My Father gives you the true bread from heaven...'

He also said, 'I am the bread of life. He who comes to me will never go hungry, and he who believes in me will never be thirsty.'

Just as we grow physically hungry and need to eat to live, so too we have a spiritual hunger that needs to be satisfied. And most of us – whatever we believe – can identify with that. Although we might not fear physical hunger and starvation, we can't feed our hunger for meaning with material goods.

Without spiritual bread, we cannot hope to fill our 'whole' selves properly. It will bring us life – a life that will never fade and die. Jesus makes a promise here that every spiritual searcher can put to the test (provided our motives are right): if we feed from the life and words of Jesus, we will never go hungry.

This claim resonates with an episode later in Jesus' life – towards the very end of it, in fact – when he shared a final meal with his followers, shortly before he was betrayed by his disciple Judas.

> We think sometimes that poverty is only being hungry, naked and homeless. The poverty of being unwanted, unloved and uncared for is the greatest poverty.
>
> *Mother Teresa*

Food and drink for the body and soul

Realizing that he was about to be captured by the religious authorities (who had been looking for a way to stop him from spreading his radical message and gathering followers), he took bread, broke it and said to his disciples, 'Take, eat: this is my body, broken for you.' In the same way, the Bible reports, he took a cup of wine, saying, 'Take, drink: this is my blood, poured out for you.'

If the metaphor of bread didn't seem powerful before, then there's no denying it now. It gains a stunning potency as the bread of life, which has come from heaven to bring us life, is 'broken' – metaphorically and literally.

Astonishingly, we can – and must – participate in this metaphor ourselves, today. That's what Christians do, symbolically, in the act of the communion. But it's not meant to be only a religious ritual. Every time we get together as a

group to eat the bread and drink wine, something greater is happening than just the sum of the parts – we are eating the very bread of life itself.

Jesus spoke of himself in other pictures, too – claiming, for instance, that he was 'living water' (he took the chance to teach a Samaritan woman – someone he wasn't, as a Jewish man, even meant to speak to – when he stopped at a well for a drink). 'Everyone who drinks... water will be thirsty again, but whoever drinks the water I give him will never thirst. Indeed, the water I give him will become in him a spring of water welling up to eternal life.' Food and drink for the body and soul.

Seeing the light

Jesus also compared himself to light as he said, 'I am the light of the world.' In the West today, where we can summon light with the flick of a switch, we may need to use our imaginations to ponder just what a life-saving and life-bringing metaphor this really is. But it isn't hard. Within the long, dark months of winter, who doesn't yearn for the brighter, warmer days of spring and summer? When the days are short, we tend to feel more gloomy, even depressed.

But imagine what it was like before the days of electricity. Light and heat needed to be created and sustained; you could never let your fire go out once it was lit.

The darkness brings danger; it hides those who are threatening, those who might do us harm. It is cold and inhospitable. Many of us, quite understandably, are naturally afraid of the dark.

Light brings life. Seeds that have lain dormant in winter soil grow up through the darkness into the warmth and the light of spring. We need light to live by, and the two – light and life – are never far apart when John writes about them. Jesus is 'the life [that] is the light of all [people]'.

Food, drink and light are the basics of our human existence. And yet even these will not sustain us forever. Jesus taught us that he is the food, drink and light of life itself, a life that lasts.

As we have seen, perhaps the ultimate summary of Jesus' teaching is the statement, 'I am the way and the truth and the life.' As we have focused in these chapters on what he means by 'truth', we begin to see that truth brings life. And that is because truth is not, according to John, simply the unveiling of knowledge. Instead, it is about the unveiling of God through Jesus. As a precursor to Marshall McLuhan, the famous social commentator, Jesus embodies the idea that the medium is the message: he is both the channel through which the truth travels and the truth himself. He is both messenger and message. And because of this, we respond to truth less by learning about it, and more by accepting it and living it in relation to others.

Jesus, in other words, is not just the one bringing the good news. *He did not come just to talk about life; he is life.*

> **In the dark, a glimmering light is often sufficient for the pilot to find the polar star and to fix his course.**
>
> *Metastasio*

Sometimes the best teachers ask questions

We are on a journey of life and faith, and as we arrive at the truth of Jesus, we depart again on the journey of following him. In other words, our search for the truth about Jesus' teaching – which sets us free – is not over once we have established a relationship with him. Instead, we continue to explore the metaphors and parables, going deeper into them, reapplying them within new contexts and new stages of our life. There is always something fresh to discover about the challenge of following Jesus into truth and life.

Jesus modelled a way of teaching – and learning – that both keeps our curiosity very high on the agenda and helps us to own the search for ourselves. He taught not just in plain words but in pictures. And he taught, not just by giving answers, but by asking questions.

It's a novel approach from a so-called religious leader. Most leaders are so determined that you believe and do the right things that they can end up losing a sense of human perspective. Prescriptive words can be empty of warmth, as they replace love with legalism, and keep watch over the letter rather than the spirit of the law.

Jesus, on the other hand, threw questions back at those who questioned him: 'A certain ruler asked him, "Good teacher, what must I do to inherit eternal life?" "Why do you call me good?" Jesus answered' (Luke 18:18–19).

On another occasion, Jesus went into the temple on the sabbath and healed a man with a withered hand. The religious leaders had been watching him closely to see if he would heal someone on the sabbath, as this – by the letter of the law – meant that he was 'working' and was therefore breaking the law. 'I ask you, which is lawful on the sabbath: to do good or to do evil, to save life or to destroy it?' he retorted (Luke 6:9).

Once, a blind beggar heard that Jesus was passing and shouted, 'Son of David, have mercy on me!' Jesus replied, 'What do you want me to do for you?' (Luke 18:39, 41).

He asked many, many questions during the three years

> So much sorrow and pain,
> still I will not live in vain.
> Like good questions never asked
> is wisdom wasted on the past.
> Only by the grace of God go I,
> go I.
>
> Ben Harper,
> 'Blessed to Be a Witness'

that he taught: why do you look at the speck of sawdust in your brother's eye and pay no attention to the plank in your own? Can the blind lead the blind? Who touched me? Who do the crowds say I am? Which of you fathers, if your son asks for a fish, will give him a snake instead? Who of you, by worrying, can add a single hour to his life? Why don't you judge for yourselves what is right? What is the kingdom of God like? Who do you say that I am?

Our question, appropriately enough, is: why? Why did Jesus, who claimed to be the Son of God himself, bother to ask questions, when he surely had all the answers to hand? Why did he not just take the chance to tell people what to do, what to think and how to act, without room for error?

Questions help us to start a relationship with God

The New Testament scholar Conrad Gempf argues that Jesus was not trying to persuade people that he was who he said he was. He wasn't interested in trying to assert his credentials or proving others wrong:

> Jesus, it seems, had no desire to become a great debater and convincer. He was not in the convincing business, he was in the provoking business. His goal seems to have been to present people with opportunities to choose. In this he was incredibly successful… He refused to talk people into following him; refused to prove who or what he was.
>
> Jesus asks a lot of questions. But he doesn't ask primarily because he wants to acquire knowledge, nor does he ask to help people realize where they stand; he asks questions in order to give occasion for a reply, in order to initiate a conversation.

While we can't, today, literally sit down and talk to Jesus in the flesh, Christians do believe that they can pray, and that Jesus, who rose from the dead three days after his execution, is listening. It is a good, human thing to pray, and any spiritual searcher worth their salt would be foolish to ignore that great conversation starter, who do you say that I am?

Questions engage us. Rather than force-feeding us a load of religious information, Jesus calls us to answer for ourselves. Sadly, religious leaders across the ages have perverted this form of teaching and become arrogant, conceited and forceful instead of conversational. But that need not stop us from conversing with Jesus – from asking questions of him and being willing to have questions asked of us.

In today's consumer culture, the customer, people say, is king. If we are not careful, we approach life as a consumer, not as a participator; as a customer, not a human creature. And consumers believe that it's their right to do the asking. If Jesus wants to sell us this religion, he'll have to come up with the right answers. But that's not his style. We can only enter the narrow path of Christ if we are willing to let someone ask some serious questions of us, and to think about how we might answer them. It's not a question of what we can get out of a relationship with God through Christ; it's a question of what we can give. It's about learning and growing and continuing the conversation, walking with the God who walked, and talking with the God who asked the most telling questions.

CHAPTER 5

The truth in suffering: finding meaning in pain

We've looked at what it means to set off along the way of Christ, and to search after the truth. But as we start to focus on how we can live a different, radical life that transforms us into more fully human beings, we need to consider why following Christ requires truthfulness – especially when we experience times of difficulty and distress. The Bible is refreshingly frank about the highs and lows of the human experience, and expresses every aspect of life through its poetry, prose and narratives. So here we explore why our search for God doesn't always yield the quick fix or the instant high, but requires faith, patience and perseverance to get us through difficult times.

Cynics tend to perceive religion in two ways: either it's a self-help course served up to make us happier, or else it's a crutch for the weak, for those who cannot face the idea of a purposeless life without higher meaning. Plenty of people 'consume' religion for these reasons, of course, or for many others besides. But anyone genuinely committed to exploring the path of Christ will find that it's not all about happiness and self-help, and it's certainly not a crutch for the weak.

Jesus never once promised that everything would instantly be all right – apart from, perhaps, his promise to the robber who was hanging next to him on a cross, who still had to die a painful death before finding out whether Jesus' words were right or not – 'Today you will be with me in paradise.' Jesus never promised that we'd get rich quick, or that all our problems would disappear in the

twinkling of an eye or the mouthing of a prayer. In fact, he predicted that many people would be persecuted for following him – and the truth is that many were and still are even today.

Bearing the scars of Christ

A relationship with Jesus inspires joy, because it brings freedom, meaning and purpose when it is fully experienced.

He promised, in fact, that 'my yoke is easy, and my burden is light'. Yet a relationship with Christ calls us to flourish and grow – to 'bear fruit' as the New Testament writers wrote – and to commit ourselves to the long journey ahead. Sometimes, we grow fastest when we encounter pain or sadness, when we face trials and difficulties. Times like these are never easy, and few of us welcome them. When we've come through the other side, we may bear the scars that testify to our troubles. Yet we will almost inevitably be wiser and better people for the experience.

Jesus did not wrap himself up in cotton wool. He lived life where it truly hurt. And today he bears the scars that testify to a bloody and painful death on a cross. The Bible says that 'by his stripes' – the lashes across his back that carved his flesh to pieces – we are healed. And when the disciple Thomas doubted that Jesus had been raised from the dead, Jesus invited him to touch his hands and his sides, to feel the holes left by the nails and the gash from the sword that pierced his side. He came back from the dead both in spirit and body, and he bore the marks of his suffering.

The apostle Paul writes about suffering for Christ and bearing the 'marks' – literally, being 'branded' for him. The word Paul uses is similar to the one we use for wearing a brand today: some of us wear Nike, some Adidas. But the marks of Christ are very different: if we are branded with Christ, we may bear scars, like Paul did, who was beaten up for his faith on more than one occasion. But we should also be branded with the values that Jesus espouses: love for God and for each other; grace, peace and forgiveness; bravery, courage and strength.

So following Jesus is not the easy option that some might believe. And the man that we try to follow was actually described as a 'man of sorrows'. He didn't come to make everyone feel good; he came about his Father's business. Anyone who follows him knows that this is serious work – it is not merely a matter of personal fulfilment or the cosmic equivalent of popping a happy pill.

For he was despised and rejected by men, a man of sorrows, and familiar with suffering... Surely he carried our sorrows.

Isaiah 53:3–4

The truth is… we don't always get it

Jesus said he was the truth, and when we get nearer to that truth, then we do indeed begin to experience freedom from the usual ways of doing things – from revenge, bitterness, anger… Yet the truth is, we don't always get it right. The truth is, we don't always fully understand. The truth is, we don't have all the right answers to everything that life throws at us. And the truth is that sometimes our experience doesn't always match up to our beliefs.

As mentioned before, the apostle Paul said that it's like seeing through a glass darkly – or peering through a fog. Some things we have to believe, even if they don't seem to square up with what we're seeing at the time. Bono of U2 once wrote a beautiful song that affirmed the light and dark shades of our journey of life and faith:

> You broke the thorns and loosed the chains,
> carried my cross and all my shame,
> you know I believe it…
> But I still haven't found what I'm looking for.

It is an honest affirmation of both faith and doubt – acknowledging the work of Christ but admitting that he is still engaged in a restless search to fully experience the truth of that statement. Even Thomas, a disciple who had been with Jesus from the start and had heard Jesus promise to return from the dead, struggled to believe that it had happened, despite the fact that Jesus was standing there in the room with him.

But the truth is, too, that the Bible is surprisingly honest about our journey with God. You don't have to compartmentalize your faith and doubt as a follower of Christ. A relationship with God will be deeply and perfectly rewarding. But the journey is not over before it's begun. We set off along the path of reconciliation, striving to become more like Christ. But the Bible is realistic about our experience of life and faith, primarily because it provokes us to face up to reality, not to turn and run from

> Afflictions make the heart more deep, more experimental, more knowing and profound, and so, more able to hold, to contain, and beat more.
>
> *John Bunyan*

it. We must embrace the darkness of life in order to experience the light.

Finding meaning in meaninglessness

Followers of Christ are therefore not engaged in an escape from this life or this world, and neither are they expected to pretend that everything is all right when it isn't. We all feel pain, we all experience sorrow, we all have times when we feel like the world is crashing down around us. And the Bible contains some of the most profound commentaries on what can only be described as the deep sense of meaninglessness that we feel so acutely every now and then.

The existentialist philosophers, such as Jean-Paul Sartre and Albert Camus, explored eloquently the apparent meaninglessness of life in their novels and plays. In a world devoid of purpose – in which we were supposed to become the masters of our own destiny through science, technology

There is no sun without shadow, and it is essential to know the night.

Albert Camus, The Myth of Sisyphus

and philosophy, but failed – what are we to do? Camus, in classic novels such as *The Outsider*, wrote of our contemporary struggle to live meaningfully in the face of *absurdité* – meaninglessness.

Yet, as the writer of Ecclesiastes says, 'There is nothing new under the sun.' In fact, scholars have linked Camus's idea of *absurdité* with the ancient Hebrew word *hebel*, which is used to its most dramatic biblical effect in Ecclesiastes. Perhaps you recognize the opening line of this book: 'Meaningless, meaningless, everything is meaningless!' Not, necessarily, the words you'd expect to hear in a sacred text.

The Bible is a deep, rich treasure of historical accounts, stories, poetry and song that rewards careful and respectful reading. Most people haven't read it – and few would probably realize that it contains great wisdom that applies to our day as much as any; especially on subjects such as despair.

The book of Ecclesiastes, which comes near to the end of the Old Testament, resonates with our time more than most. It is written by a man – most people think it was King Solomon – who had fabulous wealth and wanted for nothing. Yet all the riches and wisdom in the world counted for little when he could see that bad things happen to good people, and good things happen to bad people, and that there seemed to be no rhyme or reason or cause and effect to life. At the time when he was writing this book, his people, the Israelites, believed in one, good God. Yet Solomon's words were born of the frustration that comes from believing in a divine and benevolent being while living in a world which doesn't always bear testimony to his presence. He acknowledged that the temptation is to eat, drink and be merry, 'for tomorrow we die'. But he concludes that we should, despite our misgivings, trust God, even if it sometimes seems absurd.

Why do bad things happen to good people?

While I was studying for a degree in theology, a terrible thing happened to one of my classmates. He was a Christian; he prayed every day, read the Bible, lived a good life. One day, we learned that his pregnant wife had been run over, and both she and the baby she was carrying had been killed. It was a terrible shock for us, and, of course, a crippling blow for him. This was somebody who had followed Christ so passionately that he had devoted these three years of his life to studying the Bible and finding out more about the ways of God. A very bad thing happened to a very good person, right under the supposedly watchful eyes of a benevolent God – and we were left to wonder what on earth it was all about. None of us could possibly believe the old cliché that 'everything happens for a reason'. Neither could we accept that a good God had deliberately caused this death. It was one of those dark, dark things. Where was God? We didn't know.

The event caused some people to lose their faith. Yet those who continued to believe found great succour in the book of Ecclesiastes – a book that does not run from doubt and despair but faces it head on and stares straight into the eyes of reality itself. And this book is planted right in the

Life is difficult. This is a great truth, one of the greatest truths.

M Scott Peck,
The Road
Less Travelled

middle of the Bible. It's not that the Bible wants to promote doubt, misery and despair; we believe that God will ultimately save us from such things. But in acknowledging that we feel and experience such a tangible sense of *hebel* – of meaninglessness – at different times, it stands alongside us. There is a season for everything, the writer of Ecclesiastes tells us: a time to sow and a time to reap; a time to be born and a time to die; a time to kill and a time to heal; a time to mourn and a time to dance. The Bible reflects the gamut of human experience.

You're not alone

Another part of the Bible, the book of Psalms – songs written by the Jews to be sung together in worship of God – includes more than praises of God's strength and awesome power. Once again, these psalms, a little like the U2 song mentioned earlier, engage God in a conversation, a dialogue. They don't politely ignore the bad things that happen, or look the other way, but they shout and scream at God for letting certain things happen.

Just as we saw that Jesus asked questions in order to enter into a conversation with us, so the most God-filled writers of the Bible were not afraid to ask questions of God for the very same reason. Psalm 22 starts with a bald, terrible question: 'My God, my God, why have you forsaken me?' And these words were repeated by Jesus himself, as he was nailed to the cross. The most prayerful, spiritual, soulful and peaceful human to ever walk the planet experienced alienation from God at his greatest time of need, and he wasn't afraid to say so.

Jesus' question surely could not have been rhetorical. Even now, it shatters the complacency and politeness of middle-class church culture – which can sometimes try to paper over the cracks of life. When God abandoned Jesus to die on the cross, without rescuing him with angels or armies, he didn't absent-mindedly turn the other way. Instead, he placed himself right at the very heart of the

Anyone with eyes to see and ears to hear will know that life is terribly unfair, and that it is the ordinary person, the unimportant person, the poor person, the powerless person, in other words the vast majority of the world's population, who has to bear it all. And yet, oddly enough, most people believe in God.

Peter Cotterell,
Is God Helpless?

human condition: God embraced despair, alienation, frustration, pain and death. The Son was separated from the Father, and the Father was separated from the Son. God didn't go missing. He faced the reality of the human condition and somehow, Christians believe, overcame it once and for all, so that we would no longer have to remain separated from God, and he from us.

It remains a mystery what happened on the cross. Theologians discuss and debate the issues, church leaders preach about it, poets reflect upon it, artists paint it, film-makers continue to make moving and powerful films about it. But it remains the pivotal point in human history – a moment in time, when time stood still. It is a moment for all time, when one death would bring life; when the bond between God and humanity, which was somehow broken in ancient times, was finally mended; when the way to God was restored – the way of Christ.

God with us – in our suffering

It's a perverse story, one that no one could have dreamed up: the life-force of creation becomes a man and is born in an insignificant backwater of the Roman empire. He leads a remarkable life but then dies an ignominious and humiliating death as an outsider, an outcast, a loser. It's so perverse that the apostle Paul called it 'foolishness to the Greeks' – to the clever people of his day, to the thinkers. It doesn't make sense, not in human eyes. But the greatest works of art help us to see the world in a different way; and this, in its own way, was the greatest work of all.

In getting his hands dirty, living with the poor, drinking with the drunkards and conversing with the social lepers, Jesus brought God into the heart of human suffering. Although today it may sometimes feel as if he is absent, we know, through the life, death and resurrection of Jesus Christ, that God has been there before us. He won't always take away the pain this side of eternity, but he knows what it is like. And he is right within the deepest alienation known to any of us.

In our lives we do our best to avoid pain, discomfort and death. We have become so good at staving off suffering that we almost believe that it won't happen to us. And yet, despite our best efforts, death, disease, pain and dislocation are part of the very fabric of existence. Thank God, followers of Christ do not have to attempt to escape this life but can instead embrace it – because he first did.

Faith stands true in good times and bad

Despite the unsettling nature of the story, followers of Christ nevertheless believe it to be true. They are one hundred per cent sure that Jesus was a real, historical figure, because not only were there four Gospels written about him, but other writers and accounts verify his existence around the same time. There is, if you like, a rational side to this strange, beguiling story of the God who came to earth – or enough of one to give us hope that we are not looking at a fairy tale.

However, in both the good times and the bad, every one of us needs faith – to believe in the person of Jesus and what he claims about himself; to believe in the life to come and in the 'kingdom' that we are called to bring into being here on earth; to believe that God, somehow, is still in control, despite the floods, the disasters, the wars, the famines and the personal catastrophes that befall us.

Sometimes we need to dream dreams, when all around us seems lost. Sometimes we need a vision for the future – of a different world, whose values will have been turned upside down and inside out – so that we can transform the present. Faith is part of that process. We need faith in order to make things happen. And we need faith to find the truth.

PART THREE

The Life

When we travel along the way of Christ and search for the truth, we then begin to enter 'the life' — and start the process of being transformed into his likeness. As we become more like Christ, then — wonderfully and mysteriously — we also become more like the unique person God created us to be. In these chapters, we will look at what it means to start living the life — walking in the path of Christ.

CHAPTER 6

Starting 'the life': being transformed into Jesus' likeness

We need faith in order to make things happen. Yet before we can try to change the world around us, we have to change our own ways. This means that we must admit we're part of the problem – and until we do, we won't become part of the solution. But the good news is that we can, with God's help, start to turn our lives around. We can't do it on our own – but together, and with faith, we can dream new dreams of personal and social transformation.

Why do we continue to do bad things?

In the biblical account of creation, we read of a world in which humans lived in harmony with God, with themselves, with each other and with the rest of God's creation. Yet something happened that tore us apart from the fullness of those relationships. The Bible tells a story – a very famous story – about how a serpent tempted Adam and Eve to eat from the Tree of the Knowledge of Good and Evil – an act that was expressly forbidden by God. Whether this is a literal story or a metaphorical one, it tells of how – in an act of rebellion and disobedience towards the creator – the original, perfect context in which we were set was spoiled.

Ever since, the Bible says, creation has been 'groaning'. We have fought each other, we have not been at peace with ourselves and we have struggled with the land. Ever since, humans have seen creation as something to plunder and divide; we have lost our ancient, sacred tie with the land and become increasingly unsure of our own human identity.

We have, it seems, undergone a cosmic identity crisis. But all, as they say, is not lost…

The gospel of Christ is good news. It offers us a way back – or forwards – to God that we are all, deep down, searching for. It's not only a way to God, but a way to each other, and to our rightful place as custodians of the creation that God set us within to enjoy, to look after and to be at peace with.

So the gospel is not bad news. It's not frightening news. It's not restricting or constricting. It doesn't close down life, but opens up new possibilities. It doesn't threaten to stifle or suffocate, but to breathe new life through ageing bodies, and to set free a flow of creativity and joy that no one dares to imagine.

It's good news, for those with ears to hear. And the good news is that, through Jesus' life, death and resurrection, the relationships that have been broken – between us, God and creation – are beginning to be restored. A new world is flickering into life.

As we acknowledged previously, bad things still happen to good people. We experience pain and sorrow. We don't always understand where God is. We're not always certain that he even exists.

And yet, through faith, we set off on a journey to which Christ calls us, in which we travel purposefully and positively towards the restoration of all our relationships and a personal transformation into the people God created us to be.

It's not just a personal thing, however. As we begin to undergo our transformation, we are also called by God to help others experience that same metamorphosis, as well as to seek the refreshing and revitalizing of our wider communities and God's creation.

> **Identities are highly complex, tension-filled, contradictory, and inconsistent entities. Only the one who claims to have a simple, definite, and clear-cut identity has an identity problem.**
>
> *Sami Ma'ari*

We must first admit that we need help

Before we can begin to walk the path that leads to God, however, Christ calls us to acknowledge that we need help.

After all, we can't receive help until we admit that we need it. Alcoholics can't begin recovery until they face the fact that they have a drinking problem. We are called, therefore, to repent and ask forgiveness for the things we have thought, said and done that have gone against the commands to love God and love each other.

It's not always easy, especially within a blame culture such as our own, to admit that we have done wrong things. We cherish our human rights, and we have grown up with the sense that we should be able to do what we want, when we want. Such absolute freedom, however, always comes at a cost to others – for we are all inextricably linked. No one is an island. The smallest thing I think or do ripples, positively or negatively, across the pool of human life. If I want to play music loud at night, it will keep my neighbours up, who need to work the next morning. Our actions always have consequences, and we need to face up to those before we are able to move on.

Part of the problem – and part of the solution

Some events in the history of the world speak with great clarity about the devastating effects of our loss of innocence, our dislocation from God and thus our damaged relationships with our fellow human beings. The Holocaust is a terrifying reminder of what humans can do to other humans – not in some barbaric outpost of an uncivilized part of the world but in twentieth-century Europe. On the sixtieth anniversary of the liberation of Auschwitz, John Lichfield wrote this in *The Independent*:

> The Holocaust began three years after Walt Disney made *Snow White and the Seven Dwarfs*; twenty years before the Beatles and Swinging London. Auschwitz is part of Modern Times… All is symmetrical and orderly, the product of rational, intelligent minds – modern, Western minds.

We are not all killers, or anti-Semitic, or specifically bad people. But Jesus made it very clear that we are all, in some sense, part of the problem. We may not kill, but we can easily harbour murderous anger. We may not all commit adultery, but many people do so in their own minds, which is the same thing, according to Jesus. Even if we just choose to look the other way when bad things happen to others, we are choosing to be part of the problem.

So if we are committed to walking the spiritual path, we need to take seriously the idea that we are separated from God and to seek reconciliation. The Bible talks about 'sin'; it says that we all sin and fall short of the glory of God. But this doesn't simply mean that we do bad things. It's deeper than that – it means we live outside a relationship with God.

Sin is less about 'missing the mark', as some people describe it, and more about the need to be reconciled with God through Christ. The longer we continue without God, the further we narrow down the possibilities for living a creative, good life and for changing the world around us.

> You have heard that it was said to the people long ago, 'Do not murder, and anyone who murders will be subject to judgment.' But I tell you, anyone who is angry with his brother will be subject to judgment.
>
> *Jesus,*
> Matthew 5:21–22

Once we meet God, the floodgates of life open and streams of living water, as Jesus described them, begin to flow through us and out into others.

It is a milestone on our journey of life and faith when we see that our relationships need to be restored and that we need God's help to do this. Jesus said that it's like being born again. It's a new start, as we turn from our old ways and run, instead, towards the arms of a loving God. The parable of the Prodigal Son portrays a father who is willing even to humiliate himself by running towards us – coat-tails flapping – when we ask to be forgiven by and reunited with him. The good news is, God isn't waiting with a stick with which to beat us. He is waiting to throw us a party.

Part of the 'new creation'

Jesus said that he came to make all things new. That includes us and the rest of God's creation. Once we have decided to follow Christ, we begin the sometimes painful, frequently joyful process of personal transformation. The apostle Paul writes in 2 Corinthians 5:17–18, 'If anyone is in Christ, [they are] a new creation; the old has gone, the new has come! All this is from God, who reconciled us to himself through Christ.'

He later instructs, 'With regard to your former way of life, to put off your old self... to be made new in the attitude of your minds; and to put on the new self, created to be like God' (Ephesians 4:22–24).

As we are restored, we are also transformed. This is a mysterious process – for in one sense, we are made new straightaway and in another, we embark on a lifelong journey towards complete transformation.

At first, it may seem a strange thing to contemplate – putting off our old self and putting on a new one. But there are close, contemporary cultural parallels that might help us to understand more. The biblical idea of personal transformation has a lot in common with today's culture; yet at other, key points, it signals a radical departure.

The art of recreation

Today, we play around increasingly with our identities, drawing from media images of the rich and beautiful to recreate ourselves in the images of others. A media personality such as Madonna has undergone many transformations, and in today's postmodern context, a change of appearance equals a change of person.

Anyone who believes and follows Jesus understands that they have already undergone a mysterious transformation, to become 'new creatures in Christ'. They have been forgiven, and they have entered new life in relationship with God. Yet the journey of the new self has only just begun. Now our task, as Paul says, is to be 'transformed into the likeness of Christ'. It's a transformation that goes deeper than surface appearance: it's not just about looking like a better person or a more religious being. It's not just about minding your language or becoming more polite. It's about channelling the passion of the creator for the poor, the oppressed and the marginalized. It's about being transformed into the image of the invisible God, through Christ, who showed us the way.

As we seek to follow Christ's teaching, we are set free from our old ways and released into an entirely new way of being. The journey towards absolute fulfilment begins here and now.

Reaching your potential

Most of us would like, if nothing else in life, to fulfil our potential. We possess an innate sense that we were created to become someone or to achieve something. And we consider it a 'waste of potential' if someone is cut short in the prime of their life by illness or death, or if they fail to take the risks associated with spreading their wings and learning to fly.

There are many reasons why we fail to realize our potential. We may have depression, for example, or irrational feelings of inadequacy, or we may lack confidence. It is hard to measure our potential and whether indeed we are living up to it. Yet there is more to it than a vague idea of what you might or might not fulfil in life.

Potential, in the eyes of a follower of Christ at least, is something far-reaching. It is about becoming the person God created you to be in the first place. It is less about what you can achieve (though God, like any parent, surely takes great pride in the good things his children do) and more about the inclination of your heart.

It is about both becoming more Christlike and more fully yourself. Therefore, it goes beyond the consumerist mentality of many contemporary forms of spirituality which focus more exclusively on self-realization and self-fulfilment. We need to reach deep into ourselves, for certain, but we also need to reach out beyond ourselves if we are ever to gain a divine perspective on the lives we lead.

The apostle Paul says that we need to 'die to sin' in order to become who we really are. That means putting our own selfish desires behind us and putting others before ourselves.

We look forward to a physical and spiritual rebirth

Followers of Christ believe that they will not be fully transformed until they come face to face with God in the next life. But this doesn't promise to be only a 'spiritual' experience – it will be physical too. We press forwards with faith, believing that we will be made entirely new, in spirit and body. Yet crucially, the follower of Christ believes the process starts now.

And we experience this in two ways: we must receive new life through Christ, but we must also proactively seek to live it. The Bible says that we become new 'by faith' – in other words, no amount of 'good works' alone will get us to heaven. It is only through faith in Christ that we find forgiveness and reconciliation. And yet, once we have re-established our relationship with God through Jesus, our lives must display the 'fruits' of that relationship. We must live it out.

Like many other aspects of our relationship with God, we experience a positive tension – between the 'now' and the 'not yet', and between the idea that we must die to ourselves so that we can live and lose our life to find it. We receive life for ourselves when, selflessly, we seek to gain it for others. There is an outward compulsion to our walk with Christ. It is about seeking God and seeking to love others. And happily, within that searching, we find ourselves. That is the

Well, Jesus kissed his mother's hands, whispered, 'Mother, still your tears, for remember the soul of the universe willed a world and it appeared.'

Bruce Springsteen, 'Jesus Was an Only Son'

secret to discovering what it means to live life. The life that Jesus promised us: 'to the full'.

It's not a matter of buying a lifestyle choice, which you can throw off as soon as you get bored. It is a mission that lasts beyond a lifetime. It is a commitment, a calling, a tough decision – yet one that yields the truest form of life.

The church is ... called to be a temporal echo of the eternal community that God is.

Professor Colin Gunton

The church: transforming relationships

The Christian faith differs from other spiritualities on offer in today's religious marketplace because it focuses less exclusively on the individual. Followers of Christ don't lose their individual identities as they are changed into his likeness – they become more completely themselves, displaying (however fallibly) the traits of Christ within their own lives.

Yet relationships are key. As we seek to restore our relationship with God, we must also restore our relationships with those around us. And that is where the church – at its best – plays a crucial role.

In today's culture, where we are increasingly reluctant to join a big organization and sign up to the party, it's harder to convince people of the need to belong to a church. That's mainly because the church is often perceived as being part of the problem. If we see the church as an old, outmoded institution, then it's perfectly reasonable to think that contemporary spirituality should not be incarcerated within the dusty walls of decaying church buildings.

And yet, Jesus had different ideas for the church he said he would 'build'. It was not to be a building or an institution. Instead, it was to be a revolutionary network of believers who would support each other, help the poor and meet to worship their God together. While the importance of communal worship cannot be overlooked and dismissed, the church is not exclusively about Sunday morning worship – where the church is 'gathered' – but about the effect its

members can have on a struggling society day by day, hour by hour, while they are 'dispersed'.

The church is meant to be a transformative community of people who haven't hidden themselves away from the world but are working tirelessly and passionately to see God's values – of honesty, grace, forgiveness, reconciliation and care for the poor – changing the world around them.

Church was never meant to be a bore or a chore; it was never meant to become a tradition. It is human nature to get stuck in our ways, and some churches have done so. But the spirit of the creator God cannot, ultimately, be dammed, and there are many vibrant and exciting examples of the church in both its gathered and dispersed forms as we flow into the uncharted territory of the twenty-first century.

Going to church: negative perception or positive experience?

In some ground-breaking research among agnostics, called *Beyond Belief*, Nick Spencer of the London Institute for Contemporary Christianity discovered a big difference between agnostics' perceptions of Christians and the church and their actual experiences. Almost all of those he interviewed had a knee-jerk reaction when they were asked to describe what a Christian or a church was like. Perhaps you might react similarly. They said that Christians (and other 'religious' people) were old-fashioned, outdated and intolerant of others.

When Spencer's interviewees were asked to describe their actual *experiences* of church and Christians, their attitudes differed remarkably from their original, negative perceptions. Their feelings about the people they had encountered – perhaps when they'd had to arrange a funeral or needed support from others at difficult times – were almost exclusively positive.

It is crucial, if any spiritual searcher is to investigate seriously the claims of Christ and the church, to acknowledge the potentially damaging power of first impressions, or worse, media impressions, and to search for a genuine experience of the support and collective sense of worship within a local community of Christian people.

But it is also important for Christians to realize what image they are projecting and how their walk along the way is shaping that image. Jesus used metaphors to describe what his followers should be like in the world. They should be like salt, which preserves meat, he said. You only need a little salt to keep something from rotting. The community of his followers should act, together, as salt within the wider community.

He also said that his followers should be like light. God brings light to banish darkness. You can see a lighted match from a long way away when you are in the pitch darkness. And followers of Christ are able to point to a better way — through the example of their lives, more than by their words — within a wider community that is so frequently bored, depressed or directionless.

Following Christ is not so much about how to behave in church as how to live life more fully. It's less about how to conform to a uniform set of beliefs and behaviours, and more about finding our individual identity as people within a vibrant set of fulfilling relationships. It's not so much about fearing to miss church on a Sunday morning as not being able to wait to get back together to worship a creative and loving God.

This community of people who follow Christ is an international one, spread far across the world. The Bible describes it as a 'body with many parts'. In every country, on every continent, you will find unique communities who worship God in their own ways. Yet they are bound together with a love for God, a love for each other and a love for the world around them that speaks of a very different way of being: of sharing, caring, forgiving, supporting, encouraging, praying, singing, dancing, celebrating, transforming and living.

The church, at its best, is a transformative community in which we can find our true identities and in which we can begin to flourish. It doesn't always match its ideal

> We must be clear that our churches are not primarily hospitals for the spiritually insane, or sanctuaries for the emotionally disturbed, or refuges for the battered and bruised, but centres of pilgrimage and exploration where we seek to discover what it means to be a human being.
>
> *Colin Greene*

calling, because we are fallible beings who are in constant need of God's grace, patience and help. But it is a family of people who are willing to start the journey by acknowledging their need for such help and for each other.

CHAPTER 7

A deeper life: discovering who God wants us to be

We have been travelling on the way of Christ and learning how to have the life he offers us. In this chapter, we ask what it means to enter that life more deeply – to become more fully human and to reflect the divine imprint of the creator in how we live. It's a matter of image and identity – but not as we know it...

The person we'd like to be

Everyone is an artist, and we are all engaged in the art of image management. Whether we pop in for a haircut to recreate ourselves in the image of Jennifer Aniston or Brad Pitt, or whether we pay thousands for a nose job, a breast enhancement or a tummy tuck, we are all playing with our appearance in order to present the person we would like to be to the world at large.

In fact, within our culture, we can become more or less who we would like to be through a change of costume. If we're bored with who we are, we can undergo a metamorphosis, reconstructing and re-representing ourselves to a watching world that will readily consume our image from the outside in. In fact, we are continuously encouraged to do so through the fashion and lifestyle media, which focus almost exclusively on surface appearance. It doesn't matter whether we really are who we appear to be; for image, they say, is everything. We have myriad subcultures to explore and plunder for their subcultural

Another secret
for ya:
I've been told if
you want to
make it in this
game,
You got to have
the luck,
You got to have
the look.

The Libertines,
'The Man Who
Would be King'

trappings of clothes, books, accessories and so on. So pick your personality!

It's like surfing. We could become a 'surfer' by growing and braiding our hair, buying the surf clothes from the right shops and the right labels, talking the language of the surfing culture and basking in the reflected glow of 'cool', which accompanies the apparent lifestyle choice. We could even buy the VW camper van to complete the image. And all of this we can do quite effectively without ever having to get our feet wet, let alone learning how to ride a ten-foot wave.

And as for surfing, so it goes for all the other cultures and subcultures that are on offer in the lifestyle marketplace (including religious or spiritual ones). We are living at a time in which who you are is rapidly becoming what you wear, and this is a creative, though unsettling – and ultimately dehumanizing – state to find ourselves in.

Who am I? Is image more than skin deep?

It's dehumanizing because, along with the fashionistas who tell us to recreate ourselves as often as we like, many philosophers today suggest that we are simply a pack of clothes-horses: all surface and no depth. At best, they suggest, we are the sum of our relationships – created and recreated through who we speak to and how people perceive us. 'Being,' they say, 'is becoming.' You can never find out who you really are, because there is no 'you'. We are constantly changing, never settling, never coming face to face with the real person. We have no essence – no essential core, no ultimate 'you of you' or 'me of me'.

In other words, in today's postmodern world, we are deemed utterly soulless. We have no timeless, immutable sense of self that can anchor our innermost being in the choppy waters of contemporary life. We are the shopkeeper's mannequin personified – on which we can all drape our off-the-rack clothes.

What is the you of you, the me of me?

Douglas Coupland,
Life After God

Stop and think: who will you become?

I often wonder who is the me of me, the you of you. What links me to the little child that I was, and the old man that I am set to become? What thread, what common denominator? If I sat on the bus next to the old man I am going to become, would I recognize myself in him? Would I see something familiar in his smile, or a spark of me deep within his eyes? Would I like what he's wearing? Would I be interested in what he's reading? What would we talk about? How would his experiences have helped to shape who he is now? Would we get on? And where would he get off? Would we believe the same things?

Think about who you might become, or how you connect with the little boy or girl you once were. Is there an essence or a thread that runs throughout your life? How have your relationships shaped who you are, how you see your former self and who you are becoming? You might, alternatively, consider what you would like to see written on your gravestone – a three or four-word epitaph, that sums up who you became and who, essentially, you were. How do you wish to be remembered? And is this something you can strive for in your life to come?

The follower of Christ can acknowledge both the truth and falsehood of the old and the new philosophers. We are neither exclusively individual (as the old ones believed) nor only the sum of our relationships (as the new ones suggest). We can, instead, offer an alternative perspective: we all have a unique identity, because we have been created in the image of a diverse and multifarious God. We are 'essential' creatures, yet we are also being transformed continually through our relationships with each other, with the planet and with God. In that more wholesome sense, being is becoming, because we are being positively transformed into the people God created us to be.

Humans look at the outward appearance, but God looks at the heart.

1 Samuel 16:7

God looks at the heart

Although the peculiar pressures of a postmodern culture focus on surface and image, people have always tended naturally to judge others by appearance. It's a human thing. And the Bible, that ancient, sacred text, acknowledges this: 'Humans look at the outward appearance,' it says, 'but God looks at the heart.'

Jesus even berated the religious leaders of his day – those who should have known better – for their focus on the outer, not the inner, self. 'Woe to you,' he declared. 'You clean the outside of the cup and dish, but inside they are full of greed and self-indulgence.'

We all hate religious hypocrisy – especially today – and must take great care not to claim we are one thing (especially if it's 'Christian') while acting in the opposite way. Nevertheless, the fact that God looks on the heart is good news, essentially.

For a start, it means that God knows what we are really like, even if others can't be bothered to find out. At a time when so many of us feel pressured to conform, to look our best, to lose more and more weight (especially teenage girls) so that we comply with the unrealistic images set before us in magazines and on television, we can take heart. What you see is not what you get – God knows. God knows about our

Stop and think: Psalm 139

You might, for a moment, stop to pray the prayer from Psalm 139. And why not, as you do so, find a mirror and stare into it deeply. Ask yourself first how you see yourself. Be honest. You might like to write down what you observe.

Secondly, ask yourself how other people see you. Again, be honest. How would you judge this person in the mirror if you were passing them on the Underground, or crossing the road? Thirdly, ask how God might see you. What lies behind the face? Beyond the lines of experience that are faintly drawn in the folds of our skin? Beyond the hairstyle, or the make-up? What is the difference between the way God might see us and the way we perceive ourselves? Write down your thoughts and pray again the psalmist's words: 'Search me, O God, and know my heart.'

insecurities, our hurts, the things we suffer in silence, even if no one else seems to.

Beyond that, it also means we can affirm that there is a 'me of me' and a 'you of you', something essential that God can see and relate to. Some might call it a soul, although to restrict it to a spiritual thing is to partly miss the point. We are whole, holistic creatures, who comprise many parts – body, mind, spirit, heart and so on – and somehow, the sum is greater than the parts. God knows. God sees. And God calls us to account for who we are.

The writer of one exquisite psalm – Psalm 139 – says, 'Search me, O God, and know my heart; test me and know my anxious thoughts. See if there is any offensive way in me, and lead me in the way everlasting.'

Psalm 139 is one of the most beautiful affirmations of personal identity you could hope to find. It is worth reflecting on at greater length. As you read the following words, try to let them become more than just words on a page. Try to allow them to seep into your soul, as you reflect on the wonder of your uniqueness:

O Lord, you have searched me and you know me. You know when I sit and when I rise; you perceive my thoughts from afar… Where can I go from your Spirit? Where can I flee from your presence? If I go up to the heavens, you are there; if I make my bed in the depths, you are there. If I rise on the wings of the dawn, if I settle on the far side of the sea, even there your hand will guide me, your right hand will hold me fast. If I say, 'Surely the darkness will hide me and the light become night around me,' even the darkness will not be dark to you; the night will shine like the day, for darkness is as light to you.

For you created my inmost being; you knit me together in my mother's womb. I praise you because I am fearfully and wonderfully made; your works are wonderful, I know that full well. My frame was not hidden from you when I was made in the secret place. When I was woven together in the depths of the earth, your eyes saw my unformed body. All the days ordained for me were written in your book before one of them came to be.

The writer of Psalm 139 affirms that we have been created uniquely by God, and that – whether we want to or not – we can't escape from the loving gaze of the creator. This idea is repeated later in the Bible by the apostle Paul, who prays that his readers will grasp 'how wide and long and high and deep is the love of Christ' (Ephesians 3:18).

Such ancient wisdom cuts through today's postmodern rejection of the soul and reaffirms that, as human beings, we can enjoy a relationship with our creator.

Made in the image of God?

The Bible is not a long list of dos and don'ts. It is a mine of wisdom, which unearths insights from a people who were, perhaps, walking more closely with God than we are today. As such, it speaks from a different perspective into the very heart of contemporary issues such as identity – and it can help to take us beyond the confines of our popular culture. In other words, it can help us to grow deeper, as spiritual, physical, soulful human beings.

One unique perspective the Bible has to offer comes in the area of identity. At the very beginning of the Bible, we read of the creation of the world. Some people take this account literally; others believe that it is a story that contains truthful principles about God's relationship with humanity, and its subsequent dislocation.

The Bible records that God created humans 'in his own image'. But that is a peculiar thing to suggest, when elsewhere it talks of the 'invisible God'. How can we be created in the image of an invisible God? What does it mean? It's a fascinating question to ask, especially from within an image-saturated society such as ours.

First of all, it might suggest that we are created with similar attributes to God: that we are relational creatures who love, and who love to be loved. Biblical scholars throughout the last 2,000 years have agreed that the Bible

---

Stop and think: unique you

In a moment of quiet, you might like to sit down and look at your thumb print. It is utterly unique. In a world of over five billion souls, no one has another like it. There is no one else quite like you. No one has your precise DNA. No one sees the world in quite the way you do. Your voice counts. Your views count. You count.

Perhaps, in a moment of gentle gratitude, you can repeat the psalmist's words to your creator: 'I praise you, because I am fearfully and wonderfully made.' You might also like to reflect on what it is that makes you unique. If you were a business, what would be your unique selling point? Try writing down the things that you do really well – especially those things that you feel, deep down, that you do better than anyone else you know. If you're not sure (or too modest!), why not ask a friend to tell you what they think is uniquely strong about you? At the same time, you can do likewise for them.

presents God as a 'holy Trinity' – that is, God is 'three in one'. It is a mystery how three distinct 'persons' (for want of a better word) are part of the same being, yet Christians believe that they are. They worship God the Father (the creator), God the Son (Jesus) and God the Holy Spirit (God sent his Spirit to the world after Jesus left to return to heaven). These three are distinct, yet they relate to each other perfectly. And in a faint echo of the three-in-one God, we reflect this mystery. We are unique, distinct beings, yet we need each other to complement and complete who we really are. We exist as individual people, but our individuality is only defined within a community – in relationship. We cannot fully 'be ourselves' outside of the relationships that make us human; and yet these relationships can only flourish because we are ourselves – and, crucially, we are all different.

We all reflect something unique about God

And herein lies one of the truly heartening things about the biblical idea of God – an idea so radical that even Christians find it hard to live out, though they aspire to.

The Bible celebrates the fact that we are all individuals, because God has created us this way. Although none of us is perfect, nevertheless, in some, small way, we all reflect something singularly good about humanity. We are all distinct expressions of our race. And if humans have been created in the image of God, then amazingly, we must also reflect something unique about God's image too. We are charged with the responsibility of reflecting that unique part of God's image that shines through us.

This is a truly awesome thing to contemplate. We should not only respect ourselves and learn to love ourselves more deeply as creatures made in the image of God; we must also love our neighbours as ourselves. For they too are created in the image of a good God. They too bear God's imprint.

The Good News, as it relates to our culture, is that being fully human has been demonstrated for us in the person of Jesus Christ, made accessible to us through baptismal incorporation into his death, resurrection, ascension and the gift of the Holy Spirit, and – how wonderful it would be if we could add! – is now being incarnately demonstrated at your nearest local church.

Robert Warren, Being Human, Being Church

They too reflect the divine within the deeply flawed body of the human race – however different they may be from us. As we follow the path of Christ, we must celebrate our differences, as we also celebrate the fact that Christ unites us through – not despite – those differences. Our human impulse is often towards creating uniformity – making ourselves more like other people, or making other people more like ourselves.

The church, at its best, provides a community in which we can begin to show how to celebrate each other's differences and not demand that we all conform to a cultural stereotype. It is a community in which we can practise loving each other, and in return, learn to love ourselves as others – God included – love us.

God saw us and said that we were 'good'

Religion has often been its own worst enemy. It has sought, through good intentions, to flee 'the world, the flesh and the devil' because of the bad things that we do to each other. It has tried to help us escape the reality of our brokenness by setting us on a fast-track to heaven — and by discounting anything worthwhile in this world and this life in the process. It has focused on the damaged side of human nature and neglected the idea that we are created in the image of a good God. Yet the fact that the Bible says we are created in God's image should provide us with reason to hope: after all, although we know that we tend to do bad things and frequently let ourselves and others down through our thoughts, our words and our deeds,

Musicians give us a glimpse of what we might be of our best selves, and of an impossible world in which you give everything you have to others, but lose nothing of yourself.

Ian McEwan,
Saturday

nevertheless, we bear the imprint of the creator God.

The biblical account of creation is a wonderful affirmation of all things physical as well as spiritual. It paints a picture of a physical world that was, at the very beginning at least, in harmony with its creator. As God created the heavens and the earth, as he made the trees, the plants, the sea and land, the animals and, last of all, human beings, at each stage he reflected on his creation – 'and saw that it was good'.

While we talk a lot about original sin, we rarely talk about original blessing. But as human beings, we also have an impulse to do good – to love our fellow creatures, to put others first, to exhibit grace and forgiveness when others do us wrong and to display unwarranted love to those who do not like us. In all of these good things, the original blessing of God's act of creation breaks through.

If nobody speaks of remarkable things, how can they be called remarkable?

Jon McGregor,
If Nobody Speaks of Remarkable Things

CHAPTER 8

A life less ordinary: getting closer to God

If we're to start living the life that Jesus calls us to, we must resist the cultural desire to escape from reality, and instead, try to face it head on. We are not called to escape injustice but to tackle it; we are not called to escape our despair but to engage it; we are not called to escape our boredom but to transform it into purposeful living. In following Jesus, we choose to live. This chapter explores some of the reasons we try to escape our present situations, and looks at how creating 'sacred space' in our lives – for times of quiet and contemplation – can provide a more nourishing alternative to the white noise of the world around us. As we do so, we move closer to God, closer to each other and closer to ourselves.

In today's world, in a culture stuck on fast-forward, we often don't have the time to stop and think about how we might live differently, or better. We don't have the space. Many times, we find ourselves stuck on a treadmill that we can't get off. But we need to force ourselves to stop and take stock. To think, is this really what I want to be doing? Is this really how I want to go on living? When we sense the dislocation between how we'd like to live and how we are in fact living, we often prefer not to look life in the eye and face up to the changes we know we should make. Instead, we look for an easier way out.

We have so much – so why aren't we happy?

It's ironic for those of us in the rich West to find ourselves wrestling with depression and despair, but many of us are. The statistics are startling. Every year in Britain alone, some 13 million prescriptions are written out for anti-depressant drugs such as Prozac and Seroxat.

Of course, there are many theories as to why we find life so difficult – when most of us have never had it so good. But from a spiritual perspective, it is hardly a coincidence that our cultural malaise comes at a time when trust in organized religion is on the decline, and we are, as a culture, experiencing an overall loss of meaningful direction. It may not be the whole reason, but it certainly plays its part in contributing to our lack of purpose.

To put it simply, we're not sure why we should get out of bed in the morning. Or, as Elizabeth Wurtzel wrote in her best-selling book *Prozac Nation*, 'You wake up one morning afraid you're going to live.'

Identifying our escape routes

We are all, to one degree or other, escaping from someone or something. Whether it's through losing ourselves in the drama of 'reality TV' for nights in a row, or playing golf at the weekend to retreat from the madness of a young family, or searching for a higher, more exciting, yet dangerous plane through drugs, most of us, in our own way, use the mechanism of escape to cope with the reality of life in the twenty-first century.

Not all of us are clinically depressed or taking Prozac to keep the black dog at bay. But many people today are either bored with the routine of their lives or stressed at their

> **Stop and think: mission statement**
>
> Try to think about your *raison d'être* – your 'reason for being'. You might find it helpful to write a 'mission statement' about your life – in other words, a short summary of why you get up in the morning. If you find this hard to do, you might try talking to people you know who have a greater sense of purpose, and asking them what motivates them.

busyness. With the invention of the computer, we were promised an age of leisure in which our working hours would be greatly reduced and our time for each other and for ourselves would increase dramatically. As it happens, working hours are on the increase, and many people find themselves spending more time with their colleagues in the office than they do with their loved ones at home.

Sadly, it's often the case that our escape routes do not, in the end, provide the fulfilment we crave. They may provide happy diversions – we might get a genuine thrill from bungee jumping, we may expand our horizons by travelling or increase our education by reading – but the question remains, how might we find fulfilment in our everyday lives?

Life is happening as we speak

While we look for the next exciting moment, while we crave the next great escape, or, more basically, while we sit there waiting for life to really kick in round the next corner, we somehow lose sight of the sacredness of the ordinary, the everyday, the stuff of real life.

We may not find ourselves in our ideal job, or marriage, or geographical location – and many of us will spend much of life feeling like we're missing out. We experience a genuine tension, between embracing the beauty of the ordinary and never giving up on our dream of finding the life we were created to lead.

This is what Douglas Coupland says in *Life After God*:

I am rubbing my eyes and trying to wake up, and my hair is brushing the tabletop which is covered in crumbs and I am thinking to myself that, in spite of everything that has happened in my life, I have never lost the sensation of always being on the brink of some magical revelation – that if only I would look closely enough at the world, then that magic revelation would be mine – if only I could wake up just that little bit more...

Perhaps it's a matter of where we look, as well as how closely. Certainly, there are positive and negative ways to channel our longing. Frustration can be a powerful motivation to search for the truth, so long as we resist the urge to live our lives exclusively in the future, or in the past.

For the follower of Christ, the art of becoming more fully human – and thus more fully the people God created us to be – is in learning to live and to love within our present situation.

Searching for the secret of contentment

This doesn't mean, of course, that we blithely accept our lot without hope of bettering ourselves or our families; but it does mean that we learn, as the apostle Paul says, to 'be content whatever the circumstances': 'I know what it is to be in need,' he writes, 'and I know what it is to have plenty. I have learned the secret of being content in any and every situation, whether well fed or hungry, whether living in plenty or in want' (Philippians 4:11–12).

Followers of Christ believe that, whether we know it or not, our yearnings and frustrations are caught up in something that goes way beyond whether we have a big enough house, a fast enough car or a cool enough outfit. It has, instead, to do with a deeper, metaphysical desire: the longing to belong.

We all yearn deeply to belong

As the philosopher and theologian John O'Donohue asks, 'Why do we need to belong? Why is this desire so deeply rooted in every heart? The longing to belong seems to be ancient and at the core of our nature...

'The most terrifying image in Christian theology', he continues, 'is a state of absolute exclusion from belonging. The most beautiful image in all religion is heaven or nirvana: the place of total belonging.'

103

In the book of Ecclesiastes, the writer says, 'God has set eternity in the hearts of [people].' We have a deep, restless and unsettling drive to find our true home. This is what we all experience as we go through the drudgery of another day, as we sit there and wonder, what's it all about? As we look to the heavens and ask, is anybody there?

Our impulse to pray at difficult or even joyful times is hard to explain, but it seems that we have an innate sense of Something or Someone beyond ourselves with whom we belong, yet whom we have trouble finding.

Such a yearning for 'transcendence' – to reach out and touch something meaningful, above and beyond ourselves – often finds its outlet through religious practices. And this doesn't just mean through church. The raised hands, the singing and chanting, the feeling of collective ecstasy that you experience at a sporting event feeds this desire in a similar (and sometimes more exciting) way to your average church service.

We find other outlets too. In today's postmodern, consumer-driven context, spirituality is sold to us through books and tapes and lifestyle accessories as a form of escape. The quietness and solitude of many forms of eastern spirituality promise flight from the white noise of a culture in overdrive. But sadly, the individualist, consumerist mentality demands first and foremost that spirituality is there to serve us, and not the other way around. We can treat it as a disposable commodity, like a mobile phone, which can be traded in and upgraded as soon as we get bored. So it is rare that we go deep enough, and practise the art of stillness and silence for long enough, to really benefit. It is also less common, in alternative spiritualities, to find 'communion' with others as we also seek it with God.

> **The most terrifying image in Christian theology is a state of absolute exclusion from belonging. The most beautiful image in all religion is heaven or nirvana: the place of total belonging.**
>
> *John O'Donohue,* Eternal Echoes

Just another escape?

Karl Marx argued that the church and organized religion offered the greatest and most unhelpful diversion from reality in the world. He called it the 'opiate of the masses' — it was, to him, a form of escape that, all the while we subscribed to it, meant we wouldn't face up to the harshness of our situation (and thus be provoked into action to change it) because we were promised riches in the next life, not this one.

Back to life, back to reality.

Soul II Soul, 'Back to life'

It is a very powerful and disarming critique, and one that we should take seriously as spiritual travellers. For Marx is right in suggesting that any religion that does not bring about personal and social transformation is in the end just another form of escape.

The church has, historically, often over-emphasized the rewards of the next life in order to gain and maintain its adherents in this one. That's not to say the rewards of eternal life aren't tantalizing and beguiling; we all yearn to live forever, probably more than we want anything else. Yet life must start now. And when it does, and as we begin to experience the joy of becoming more fully human, the world around us begins to change, for good.

That's because the follower of Christ cannot escape from reality. The escape, instead, is towards reality — in all its sorrow and joy, in all its pleasure and pain. Jesus didn't come to drag people away from the dirty business of living life; he came to help us live it better, and to the full. As we come face to face with Jesus, we must also come face to face with our own lives.

Seeing life from heaven's perspective

This involves being honest about who and what we are, as we have already thought about — and being willing to repent and turn away from our destructive natures. But it also means that we are liberated to show how life can and must be different — through the transforming power of love in our relationships with each other, with God and with the planet. The waiting is over: life has already begun.

And so, as followers of Christ, we gain two perspectives on life, for we are able to see this present life in relation to

eternity. Our citizenship is in heaven, says Paul – a place where all things will be made new, where our relationships will be fully restored and where our longing will turn to full belonging. And yet we become 'ambassadors for Christ' – for a different, positive way of living, here on earth.

Retreating to the quiet places

But in order to keep things in perspective, we have to be able to find the time and peace and space in which to reflect on our lives. Jesus showed us how to live. As followers of Christ, we are able to see the example set by God – the God who became human to walk in our footsteps and help us walk in his. He became fully immersed in the stuff of life – getting involved in the pain and hurt and frustration of people's daily lives, and experiencing plenty of hurt and frustration for himself. But he also withdrew to the quiet places, to counter the white noise of his own culture. Frequently, he went out to deserted places to pray and to seek after God.

We can learn much from this 'holistic' approach to life. Our spiritual walk is not entirely based upon 'zoning out' the noise around us; yet neither is it entirely based upon changing the world through busyness and endeavour. We need to strike a balance. And within an increasingly noisy, busy world, we need, perhaps, to try harder to carve out 'sacred space' for ourselves, for each other and for God. We need to start practising the art of stillness, and learning that less is frequently more.

There are many ways of trying to strike this balance – but one practical, middle way between escape from the negative pressures of this world and the hard work of transforming them is through spiritual discipline. And 'ascetism' – the act of living simply and occasionally denying ourselves the luxury of material things – is a useful place to start.

Ascetism has had a bad press. 'In its most intense form,' writes John O'Donohue, 'the ascetical mind was very bleak and engaged in a radical denial of self and the world.' In other words, it's often been associated with an unhelpful desire to punish ourselves and to retreat from this world entirely. Its more balanced expression, he suggests, seeks to change the way we try to define ourselves solely through our possessions, achievements and power.

'Much of contemporary life suffers from a vast over-saturation. We have so much, that we are unable to acknowledge or enjoy it.' Banks, O'Donohue points out, buy Van Gogh paintings as investments, as 'products', and end up storing them in their vaults where no one can enjoy them.

It's always very hard to choose willingly to deny ourselves. Yet when we do, we often experience greater freedom than when we exercise our freedom to acquire things. The challenge, perhaps, is to build an element of the ascetic into our normal, everyday lives – in the same way that shopping has become second nature to us, for example.

It would buy us, instead, a sense of space, and help – in O'Donohue's poetic words – to make 'clearances in the undergrowth of banality and sensation' which leaves us so distracted and overwhelmed.

It's time to confront the void

Whether it's an insatiable desire to shop, or to work and keep busy, to watch endless TV, or to lose ourselves on the computer, most of us are, if we are honest, afraid of 'nothingness' – of that moment when we have to stop and confront our true selves and our real situation. (Most of us are probably so busy that the one time we cannot escape this time is when we go to bed and lie awake thinking…)

Yet as followers of Christ, we are called to face nothingness with greater confidence – head on, in fact – and turn it into stillness, clarity, contemplation and meditation. We can use it to centre ourselves, as we focus on drawing closer to the God who lives and breathes through his creation and creatures.

Any spiritual 'discipline' is difficult; we all have to learn to walk a few first steps on the path of self-denial. But it need not be overwhelming: if you see one day as a microcosm of your life, you might see what you could do differently. If your life consisted of just one day, would you watch two soap operas, or spend all evening on the computer surfing the Internet?

You could try factoring into the rhythm of your week some little practice – fasting from food on a particular day, for example, trying to grow easier with your self, allowing your beliefs to be stretched and challenged and renewed.

Stop and think: making a clearing

Many of us try to give up something for Lent. It helps, in a small way, to cut a clearing within that 'undergrowth of banality' that O'Donohue writes of. Think about the last time you gave something up. How did it make you feel? Once you'd got over the initial shock, did you feel better for it?

On a camping holiday in France with my wife, it dawned on us as we arrived at our destination – a forest – that we would have no TV for a fortnight. It took a while to adjust to the fact that we needed to talk, to enjoy each other's company, to find alternative ways of spending time. In the end, we developed a routine each night of eating supper outside and then settling down, with a bottle of wine, to play Scrabble (it was the only game we'd taken with us). Through accident rather than design, we had found a space, a clearing, in our lives, which we cherished and which helped us grow closer together for two wonderful weeks.

Perhaps there is something that takes up much of your time, yet doesn't help you or the people around you to grow. Are there any simple steps you can take to change this habit? What one thing might you do differently, to start clearing the undergrowth of your life?

And as you focus inwards, you might also think about looking outwards, too – resolving to visit someone who is sick, or an elderly care home, for example, once a week. At the end of the day, the idea is not to become an introspective hermit, detached from the goings-on of the real world. It is to foster compassion, to free yourself to love God and to love others as yourself.

Developing the art and act of prayer

Spiritual discipline is not all about denial. It is a positive step towards reopening a relationship with God. And one of the most common forms of developing and nurturing your relationship with God is through prayer.

It's like any other relationship – it requires communication in order to flourish and go deeper. Most of us admit to praying, especially if we are in trouble or we need something very badly. But prayer can go far beyond the act of shooting up an arrow to the Almighty. It is, instead, the act of coming closer to the divine source of all life, coming in line with the power and creativity that flows from the creator, and drawing deeply from God's ever-flowing river of forgiveness, restoration and purpose.

Prayer can take many forms; it need not just be about words. Prayer can be taking a walk, or painting a picture. Prayer can be writing a poem, or sitting quietly with your hands outstretched or upturned. It can be feeling the smooth curves of a stone on the beach, or the rough edges of bark on a tree.

In any form, prayer has a crucial part to play, not only in helping us slow down and reflect but also in helping us draw closer to God. It almost always yields results – not necessarily in the ways we'd hope for, but frequently in ways that surprise and delight us. It helps us to find a sense of calm and well-being – and it nurtures what the apostle Paul describes as a 'peace that surpasses all understanding'.

Jesus told his disciples that the loving God – a heavenly

Father – listens to our requests and wants to help us. 'Ask and you'll get,' he said. 'Seek and you'll find. Knock and the door will open... If your little boy asks for a serving of fish, do you scare him with a live snake on his plate? If your little girl asks for an egg, do you trick her with a spider?... Don't you think the Father who conceived you in love will give the Holy Spirit when you ask him?' (Luke 11:9, 11–13)

We need to ask God to show us who he is and what he's like. If we really want to meet him, we only have to ask.

CHAPTER 9

Life to the full: strength for the journey

Every new beginning is another new beginning's end. And as we approach the end of this short journey of exploration, it is time to contemplate setting off again and moving on. In this chapter, we look at what it means to 'remain' in God, and what can hold us back from living life to the full. We'll take some last looks at the way Jesus walked the path, and answer some important questions for the road ahead: how do we travel 'light'? How do we move on from here? And how do we follow Jesus' lead? Can we learn to let go and to see the world again through the eyes of a child?

This is not the end, but the beginning – of a life of wonder and adventure as a follower of Christ.

Remaining in Jesus, leaving the world behind

It's hard to know where to start when you want to live a better, more fulfilling life of purpose and destiny. You have little time for yourself, let alone others. But in Jesus' words and life, we have a starting point. He doesn't expect us to change our lives – and the world around us – on our own. And for that reason, when Jesus left this world, God sent the Holy Spirit – the third member of the Trinity – to give us strength, to keep us going and to help us to live as Jesus asks us to.

In fact, Jesus says that we can achieve nothing through our own strength, which is heartening. Our job is to 'remain in him' – to persevere in our walk along the way, to keep the conversation going and to pray that we are filled

Blessed is the [person] whose delight is in the law of the Lord… They are like a tree planted by streams of water, which yields its fruit in season and whose leaf does not wither.

Psalm 1

with the Spirit of God. Jesus used the analogy of a vine in a vineyard. 'I am the vine; you are the branches,' he said. 'If you remain in [me] and I in [you], [you] will bear much fruit; apart from me, you can do nothing.'

Jesus knows what he's talking about. He knows what it is like to wrestle with human weakness and fallibility. So anything he calls us to do is not unrealistic – he's been there and done it himself. He experienced what it was like to be caught in a battle between walking the narrow path and going with the flow of the world; between selfish thoughts and ambition, and the distinctive life God calls us to live.

Jesus has walked the path before us

When Jesus withdrew for forty days to fast in the desert before he started his ministry, the Bible says that the devil (who may or may not be literal in this account) came to tempt Jesus with the idea that he could turn stones into bread so that he could feed himself. He then took Jesus, in his mind, to the top of the temple in Jerusalem and whispered that he could throw himself off, so that he could

be saved by angels and prove that he was the Son of God once and for all. (Then everyone would believe!) He also took Jesus to a mountain top and told him that all of the land he could see could be his, as long as he knelt to worship Satan, not God.

'Man can not live on bread alone,' he told the devil when he felt the pangs of hunger deep within his belly. 'It is written, you shall not put God to the test,' he replied when tempted to prove to the world who he was through one great, miraculous act. 'Worship the Lord your God alone, with your heart and mind and strength,' he retorted when tempted to gain the world but lose his soul by turning his back on God.

God knows. He knows what it is like to feel weak. He knows what it is like to love and to be loved. (He shared three years with twelve close friends and an entourage of helpers and devotees.) He knows what it is like to be let down. He knows what it is like to celebrate, to eat and drink and be merry. He knows what it is like to be betrayed by a close companion. He knows what it is like to be unfairly tried. He knows what it is like to feel terrifying fear (the Bible says that he sweated blood before his death). He knows what it is like to suffer when he hasn't done anything wrong. And he knows what it is like to die in someone's place.

He knows this path well.

The path to God is open for us all

In becoming a man, God took part in history's greatest act of empathy. No one could ever accuse him of being distant again. And yet the incarnation – God becoming flesh – goes deeper than pure empathy. The God we turned our backs on in Eden came to offer reconciliation. Jesus knew that he would have to die, once and for all, so that somehow, the road to the Father would be open to everyone. Look where it got him, people had taunted, as he hung on the cross. It got him all the way to us.

'For God so loved the world', says the Bible, 'that he gave his one and only Son, that whoever believes in him shall not perish, but have eternal life' (John 3:16). God is love, and Jesus was God's love incarnate. It was love that made Jesus stand firm in the face of Pilate. It was love that drove him on to his death, to save us from ourselves.

If we choose, we can follow this leader – a leader who walks with us, who does not abuse his position, act hypocritically, shout from the sidelines, put his people down, store power for himself or ask his followers to do bad things in his name; a leader who just asks us to do what he did: to love, to forgive and to serve.

> Though we dared not look on his face we could look on his fruits; and by his fruits we should know him.
>
> *GK Chesteron, The Everlasting Man*

Following his lead: love and forgiveness

Jesus commands us not only to love God and the people who love us. He says that we must love our enemies too. That's an easy sentence to read but a tough one to carry through. We are called to love the terrorists who would kill us in the name of their cause. We are called to love the thief

---

Stop and think: the Forgiveness Project

Andrew Rice, whose brother died on 9/11, met the mother of one of the hijackers to try to understand why his brother had been killed, and then to forgive.

He is now part of the Forgiveness Project – a movement established to tell quieter, less well-publicized tales of reconciliation; of people like him 'who have discovered that the only way to move on in life is to lay aside hatred and blame'.

Eric Lomax, a POW in Japan, found the same. He tells of how he met one of his torturers after fifty years: 'He was trembling and crying,' he said. 'I had come with no sympathy for this man, and yet, through his complete humility, he turned this around.'

It's not our place to tell those who have suffered so terribly what they should do. But neither, perhaps, is it our job to seek revenge on their behalf. As Rice says, 'Those people crying loudest for retribution so often seem to be the least affected.'

It's the hardest thing in the world to forgive our enemies. But it's not impossible. Some of the stories told by the Forgiveness Project show that Jesus' words are not empty dreams or harsh commands – but true, great wisdom for the journey of life and faith.

who wants to burgle our house. We are called to love the man behind the wheel who is causing our frustration to boil over into road rage.

'To you who are ready for the truth,' Jesus said, 'I say this: love your enemies. Let them bring out the best in you, not the worst. When someone gives you a hard time, respond with the energies of prayer for that person. If someone slaps you in the face, stand there and take it. If someone grabs your coat, gift-wrap your best coat and make a present of it... Live generously' (Matthew 5:38–48).

Jesus may have preached forgiveness, but he demonstrated it too. When on the cross he cried out for God to forgive his killers, he showed powerfully what it really meant to love your enemies. He was, after all, dying so that they might live.

His motivation was love: love for God and love for his neighbour. The very things he wants us to do, he did himself, to perfection.

Following his lead: love and service

Shortly before he died, Jesus did something very strange in the eyes of his disciples. He washed their feet. Washing feet was not odd in itself, in a culture where people wore sandals and roads were dirty and dusty. But it was an act that servants performed for their masters, not the other way around. His disciple Peter protested, saying that it was wrong for a leader to wash the feet of his followers. 'You do not understand,' said Jesus. 'You address me as "Teacher" and "Master", and rightly so. This is what I am. So if I, the Teacher and Master, washed your feet, you must now wash each other's feet. I've laid down a pattern for you' (John 13:12–15).

If we stop to reflect, the idea of an all-powerful God washing our feet can be disarming. If we give ourselves time

> **Stop and think: follow the pattern**
>
> You may not want to wash someone's feet, but try doing something that you feel is 'below' you in order to serve someone else. You may never have cleaned out the toilet at home, for example. Perhaps this is the time. You may never have made the effort to speak to the cleaners at work, or to a lowly post-boy. But these are the people for whom Jesus had the most time – the people most of us pass by and ignore...

to consider the beauty of God coming to live among us, with no possessions, in poverty, we may yet respond as God hopes: in love. Love for this God, for this man, love for his words – and love for his humble, challenging ways.

Love will change us. As our hearts warm to the love of the creator, we are not called to a life of static contentment but of ongoing purpose. That's when the hard work begins, not in our own strength but with the Spirit's help.

Travelling light and letting go

By telling us to love and to forgive our enemies and to serve each other, Jesus was calling us to live a humble life. He also spoke about guarding what we treasure most in life. 'Don't hoard treasure down here where it gets eaten by moths and corroded by rust or – worse! – stolen by burglars. Stockpile treasure in heaven, where it's safe from moth and rust and

burglars. It's obvious, isn't it? The place where your treasure is, is the place you will most want to be, and end up being' (Matthew 6:19–21).

The artist Michael Landy, in 2001, held an exhibition at the disused C&A store in Oxford Street – in the heart of London's shopping district. It was called Break Down. He gathered and catalogued everything he owned, and then systematically dismantled his possessions and ground them down before the public's eyes. There were 7,226 items to destroy. When it ended, he was left with nothing.

That's not *exactly* what Jesus means by saying that 'whoever finds life will lose it, but whoever loses it for my sake will find it' – but it was hard, watching each item clatter along a conveyor belt towards destruction, not to glimpse a little of what Jesus may have meant. As we accumulate more and more things around us, it becomes more and more difficult to get to the heart of true, free living.

The more we have, the tighter we hold on to it. The more we have, the harder it becomes to give it away and to 'live generously'. Landy made everyone who came to view his exhibition think hard about the value of their possessions, and their relationship to them. Unless we hold lightly to what we have, we can soon become enslaved to it. There are certainly more important things to strive for in life. After all, we enter the world naked, with nothing, and depart from it as we came.

It's a matter of what might stop us from ultimately following Christ, and we have to make ourselves confront this possibility with honesty. A rich young man once asked Jesus what he must do to inherit eternal life. Jesus told him to sell his possessions and follow him. The rich young man left, dejected.

Jesus doesn't call everyone to sell their possessions to follow him – but in this young man, he identified the true motivation of his heart. He wanted to receive everlasting life, but he didn't want to count any cost in the process. His wealth would always come first.

> **Stop and think: obstacles**
>
> What might stop you from searching for true life? What might hinder you from truly searching after the way of Christ? What, in your life, is most precious to you? If your house was burning down, what would you try to save first? Why? Could you do without it?
>
> As an act of 'letting go', why not go through your wardrobe and clear out some of your excess clothes? Give them away to a charity shop or homeless shelter. Try to live with a smaller wardrobe, and next time you are tempted to buy something new for the sake of it, or out of habit, give the money you would have spent to a local charity instead.

The faith of a child

Living humbly can be difficult, and even Jesus' disciples found it hard. At one point, they started arguing over which one of them would be most famous. 'When Jesus realized how much this mattered to them, he brought a child to his side. "Whoever accepts this child as if the child were me, accepts me," he said. "And whoever accepts me, accepts the One who sent me. You become great by accepting, not asserting. Your spirit, not your size, makes the difference"' (Luke 9:47–48).

Children play an important role in the teaching and life

It occurs to me that all the contorted theories about Jesus that have been spontaneously generating since the day of his death merely confirm the awesome risk God took when he stretched himself out on the dissection table – a risk he seemed to welcome. Examine me. Test me. You decide.

Philip Yancey,
The Jesus I
Never Knew

of Jesus; so much so, in fact, that he says we must become like a child again if we are really to enter a relationship with God properly. It's an appropriate thought with which to conclude the end of this short journey along the way of Christ.

One day, Jesus' disciples tried to stop a group of children getting through the crowd to see him: 'Jesus was irate and let them know it: "Don't push these children away. Don't ever get between them and me. These children are at the very centre of life in the kingdom. Mark this: unless you accept God's kingdom in the simplicity of a child, you'll never get in" ' (Mark 10:14–15).

Jesus doesn't mean that we should remain as children for the whole of our lives. We need to grow in maturity, wisdom and truth. Yet the attitude in which we approach God should always be childlike: filled with awe, wonder, spontaneity, creativity, playfulness, trust and acceptance. Jesus demonstrated his dependence on God the Father by praying to him and trusting in him for help, strength and wisdom. We'd do well to do likewise, if we want to learn what it means to become a 'child of God'.

For all the wisdom in the world, we must come to God

Stop and think: through a child's eyes

My father used to take me to watch soccer in Brighton. Brighton and Hove Albion were an up-and-coming team who attracted biggish crowds, and as a child, my first experience of it all was overwhelming: the sights, smells and sounds of a real, 'live' soccer stadium were like nothing I had ever experienced before. Several years later, I returned to the stadium and was surprised at how small it seemed compared with my memories of the place. I was disappointed at how tame the atmosphere was, how unimpressive the spectacle.

Think of a place or an event that you attended when you were a young child – one that really thrilled you and filled you with excitement. Now think how your attitude might be different if you returned to it. What has happened to your perception of it? What might contribute to your feelings of anticlimax?

first to receive his love, like a child would receive the love of their mother or father.

Now think of an 'everyday' object that you might be tempted to take for granted. A simple flower, perhaps. A sunrise. A colourful balloon. Try to see it as you would have the first time. Try to notice things you wouldn't normally – the minutiae of detail that only a child would spot. Stop to sense the childlike wonder of seeing the world through fresh eyes. You might like to respond creatively, as a child would – by painting a picture, making a collage or modelling some clay. You could surprise yourself with your creativity!

Finally, try to imagine meeting Jesus, as if, perhaps, you were one of those children who were pushing through to see him. Release your grip on the unhelpful images of religion and religiosity that have grown around him over 2,000 years and try to see him, like a child, for the first time. What might he look like? What might his voice sound like? How does he differ from your original perception?

We are not consumers of this world – we are in communion with it

Jesus was always turning conventional wisdom on its head when he spoke, and he turned the world upside down through his life, death and resurrection. Much of what he said needs careful, patient unpacking, for example, 'The first shall be last and the last shall be first'. We might sense what that could mean, that those on the margins – the forgotten people, the misfits, the homeless, the downtrodden – might be the first through when God opens the doors to heaven. But the follower of Christ will spend a lifetime praying, reading, reflecting and trying to become more like him in the process. It's a long haul. We must return, time and again, to his teaching, to his parables, to inhabit and explore his metaphors and to recall the example of his life.

Everything along the journey points to reconciliation, restoration and relationships. The Archbishop of Canterbury, Rowan Williams, recently wrote an introduction to a Church of England discussion paper on the environment (called 'Sharing God's Planet'). And in his notes was buried a small phrase that helps to sum up our place on planet earth at the onset of the twenty-first century.

'We are not consumers of this world,' he wrote. 'We are in communion with it.' In other words, we are not here to take what we can from life, from the world around us and from other people. We are here, instead, to live in balance; to form good relationships in which we bring what we can to others and receive what they have to bring to us.

Neither are we consumers of religion, but we are in communion with God. He is not another twenty-first century commodity, to be bought and sold at will. He is not an icon of cool to wear as a silhouette on a T-shirt. He is not here to serve our every need, although he chose to serve our deepest needs willingly and freely.

Freely we can receive. Freely we can give – to God, to others, to the world around us, to our enemies, even. The way of Christ is good news to those who travel along it. And in today's world, it's especially good news. We can receive freedom, identity, relationship and fulfilment. All of this came at a cost – the life and death of Jesus Christ – that we couldn't afford. But it's been given to us for free.

And our response? If we're serious, we'll search after the God who made life possible; we'll search to the full and try to live to the full, despite the setbacks, the times when life crashes in around us, the doubts and the disasters. In fact, within those times especially, we'll search for the God who searched for us first, and who waits within the mess for us to find him.

As we glimpse that divine, human face, the words are already waiting on his lips: follow me. We are going on a journey.

'Not that I have already obtained all this, or have already been made perfect,' says Paul. 'But I press on to take hold of that for which Jesus Christ took hold of me… I will press on towards the goal to win the prize for which God has called me heavenwards in Christ Jesus.'

Picture Acknowledgments

Picture research by Zooid Pictures Limited.

AKG – Images: p. 66.

Alamy: pp. 12, 23, 27, 37, 58, 123.

Bridgeman Art Library: pp. 13, 118–119.

Corbis UK Ltd.: pp. 9, 14, 21, 25, 31, 33, 44, 46, 55, 59, 69, 71, 79, 80, 85, 90, 93, 94, 104, 105.

David Alexander: p. 114.

Digital Vision: pp. 60, 98–99, 107, 111, 112–113.

Rex Features: pp. 81, 120.

Sonia Halliday Photographs: p. 40.

Susanna Burton: pp. 48, 52, 97.